THE SELF-MANAGEMENT PSYCHOLOGY SERIES
Carl E. Thoresen, Ph.D., *General Editor*
Stanford University
This series of self-help books presents techniques that really work
based on scientifically sound research.

Designed with the layman in mind, each book presents a step-by-step
method you can readily apply to solve real problems you confront
in everyday life. Each is written by a respected behavioral scientist
who has achieved success in applying these same techniques.

BOOKS IN THE SERIES

Arnold P. Goldstein, Ph.D.,
Director of the Syracuse University Center
for Research on Aggression,
is a professor at Syracuse University
and has written several books and articles
dealing with behavior change, skill training,
and psychotherapy,
including a Spectrum Book entitled
*I Know What's Wrong, But I Don't Know
What to Do About It.*

Alan Rosenbaum, Ph.D.,
is an assistant professor at Syracuse University.
His major interests include
marital violence and behavior modification.

Prentice-Hall International, Inc., *London*
Prentice-Hall of Australia Pty. Limited, *Sydney*
Prentice-Hall of Canada, Ltd., *Toronto*
Prentice-Hall of India Private Limited, *New Delhi*
Prentice-Hall of Japan, Inc., *Tokyo*
Prentice-Hall of Southeast Asia Pte. Ltd., *Singapore*
Whitehall Books Limited, *Wellington, New Zealand*

ARNOLD P. GOLDSTEIN
ALAN ROSENBAUM

AGGRESS-LESS
How to turn anger and aggression into positive action

Prentice-Hall, Inc., Englewood Cliffs, New Jersey 07632

Library of Congress Cataloging in Publication Data

GOLDSTEIN, ARNOLD P.

    Aggress-less: how to turn anger and aggression into positive action.

    (The Self-management psychology series)
    (A Spectrum Book)
    Bibliography: p.
    Includes index.
    1. Aggressiveness. 2. Anger. 3. Interpersonal relations. I. Rosenbaum, Alan. II. Title. III. Series.
BF575.A3G64   152.4   81-13988
                                AACR2

ISBN 0-13-018739-9 {PBK.}

ISBN 0-13-018747-X

A SPECTRUM BOOK

Printed in the United States of America.

10   9   8   7   6   5   4   3   2   1

Editorial/production supervision by Claudia Citarella
Manufacturing buyer: Cathie Lenard

This Spectrum Book is available to businesses and organizations at a special discount when ordered in large quantities. For information, contact Prentice-Hall, Inc., General Publishing Division, Special Sales, Englewood Cliffs, New Jersey 07632.

Contents

Preface

This book deals with aggression problems—either your own or someone's close to you. It is a book of methods, showing in detail how you can handle your own aggression and help others do likewise. Psychological research has discovered and carefully refined methods in order to help you reduce the level of aggressive behavior and know what to do instead. Thus, this is a book of both aggression reducers and aggression alternatives. Follow the procedures spelled out and you will learn how to relax, control yourself, and calm down. You will also learn how to calm others down, talk with them constructively, negotiate your differences, reward their positive behaviors and inhibit their negative behaviors, and use a host of useful skills to keep your own or the other person's level of aggression in check.

Aggress-Less was written for husbands and wives, boyfriends and girlfriends, parents and children, employers and their employees, and others who interact regularly in close personal or working relationships. In other words, aggression control and aggression alternatives are essentially the concern of everyone. If you, or those close to you, are frequently angry, aggressive, or hostile; are frequently verbally abusive—yelling, shouting, arguing; or are frequently physically abusive—shoving, slapping, punching, this book is for you.

chapter one

Introduction

Jim and Helen Burns have been married for almost three years, three very stormy years. Their engagement had been short and, during the three months it lasted, there were only a few signs of the troubles to come. Jim lost his temper a few times, squeezed Helen too hard in anger once, but mostly they got along well. Since their marriage, however, things have gone downhill. Along with problems concerning money, in-laws, and sex, have also come more problems dealing with anger. Jim yells more often and, it seems to Helen, for less and less reason. He has hit her on three separate occasions in the last six months. Helen still loves him, but is increasingly afraid of him.

Barbara Parks doesn't know where to turn. She feels almost helpless in trying to manage her sixteen-year-old son, Tom. The last two or three years have been awful. Tom is doing poorly in school because he rarely studies and just seems to hang around with his friends most of the time. He's been in trouble with police once. Barbara, his mother, knows he uses pot regularly, and fears he'll get into harder drugs. She knows he is no stranger to alcohol. Mostly, she has seen Tom change over the past few years, becoming more self-centered, less considerate

1

of other people, and more "into himself" and his immediate needs. Barbara and her son have drifted further and further apart. She almost feels as if there is a wall between them. When they do talk to each other, as often as not it becomes an angry shouting match. She has sought advice from her friends, her physician, her clergyman, and read at least a dozen books, but Tom's behavior has hardly changed at all. Barbara is growing desperate.

Fred Harris and Charlie Black seem to keep rubbing each other the wrong way. Both are salesmen for Acme Products and, if it wasn't for the fact that both of them can sell pretty well, they would have been fired months ago. Maybe good salesmen are naturally competitive and overassertive, but when it spills over into out-and-out aggression, there's a problem. Fred and Charlie argue, mostly over what seem to be little things blown out of proportion—work schedules, office gossip, space, and things like that. Sometimes their arguments do get out of control with yelling, stomping feet, slamming desks, and even some pushing and shoving. Ben Johnson, their boss, is concerned that a fist fight may not be far off. He's also concerned about the effects their arguments may have on the rest of his employees. He knows he'll have to do something, and soon.

A married couple, a mother and her son, two salesmen in an office—three examples of aggression in everyday life. Also three examples of the very great difficulty people have in both controlling their aggression and in finding other, more effective means of dealing with the frustrations and problems we all face. We will return to the Burns's, to Mrs. Parks and her son, and to Ben Johnson and his fighting salesmen a number of times in this book, and use them to illustrate the two main purposes of this book.

The first is to describe, in specific detail, a series of effective methods you can use to reduce aggressive behavior, either in yourself or in other people. We call these *aggression controls.* Thus, this book contains chapters describing techniques you can use to relax and feel less tense, to control your anger and aggression, to calm yourself or others, and other means of reducing or eliminating aggressive behavior. But the reduction or removal of aggression is often not enough. Aggression controls help you and others know what *not* to do, but not what you or they should do instead.

We will also describe *aggression alternatives,* a number of methods which do not involve aggression for accomplishing positive goals. These alternative methods include the ability to carry on constructive, solution-reaching communication; to negotiate effective compromises in conflict situations; to draw up and carry out behavior change contracts, which help keep aggression reduced and solutions effective; to use rewards and punishments in such ways that alternatives to aggression increase, and aggression itself decreases; and techniques for learning a wide variety of positive skills for getting along with others nonaggressively, while still accomplishing your goals.

In teaching you and others aggression controls and alternatives, this book will try to help you learn to avoid either the extreme of aggressive behavior or the opposite, that is, being overly passive, denying that conflict can exist, or turning the other cheek too often. Just as we feel that aggression is a harmful and ineffective way for you or others to change behavior or obtain satisfaction, so is passivity. Although we urge against yelling, shouting, hitting, and all other harmful aggressive expressions of anger throughout this book, we feel opposite responses can be every bit as harmful to effective and satisfying living. Avoiding aggression by acting in very passive ways in which you, or others you are close to, quietly deny conflict at almost any cost, evade confrontation, and walk on eggs to reach a false and empty peace is clearly an ineffective and unhappy way to live. This book, in urging you and those you interact with to avoid either extreme, whether it be aggression or passivity, tries to steer a middle road. In our view, the most effective and satisfying relationships at home, work, school, or elsewhere occur when those involved are both honest and skilled. Honest and open about their feelings, needs and aspirations. Skilled in being direct, assertive, able to problem solve, and especially in the host of other aggression controls and alternatives whose description makes up most of this book. Such an individual is able to respect and actually meet his or her own needs, and those of others, by behaving in nonaggressive, nonpassive, positively constructive ways.

The aggression controls and alternatives described in the chapters which follow are all methods that have their roots in sound psychological research and practice. Aggression control fads come and go, such as screaming, crying, public confrontation, hitting one another with pillows, group games and exercises, and a variety of other flashy but largely ineffective activities. Such methods have little place among serious efforts to aid people struggling with their own or another's aggression. The methods this book contains will work for many people, most of the time. But they will only work if they are taken seriously, learned carefully, and applied energetically even if the going remains rough for a spell. Even then, a few readers may also need the help of a psychologist or another trained professional in managing their aggressive behavior and learning to use alternatives.

The order of the chapters and their topics in this book have been selected and arranged to be most helpful to you. If you and your spouse, child, or friend are locked in an aggressive encounter, the first step toward a solution is cooling down. Whoever is hot and angry—you, the other person, or both—it is important to realize that nothing constructive will happen until the levels of emotion and raw anger are reduced substantially. If it is you who are angry and aggressive, start with the methods described in Chapter 2, "Relaxation," and Chapter 3, "Self-Control." In these two chapters you will learn how to calm down; relax; actually feel less tense, irritated, and angry; and how to say things to yourself that will help you stay relaxed and less angry. Sometimes, that's all you will need to do. Calming yourself or the other person, or both, may be sufficient to get you both back on the track. But a great many times calming down will only be a beginning, the step necessary to help you begin moving toward the constructive, problem-solving steps that follow.

Once you are reasonably calmed down through using these relaxation and self-control methods, you will still have to help the other person become calm before the two of you can begin communicating in a more or less rational and constructive manner. Thus, in Chapter 4, "Calming Others," you will learn how to model calmness yourself, encourage nonangry talking, listen openly, show understanding, offer reassurance, and take other steps aimed at cooling down the aggressive person with whom you are dealing.

Constructive communication is the focus of Chapter 5, a crucial chapter in your aggress-less efforts. Relaxation, self-control and calming the other person are very important preparation steps, for the direct, solution-oriented communication this chapter seeks to teach. A dozen constructive communication techniques are carefully and fully described and illustrated, all aimed at helping you and the other person or people reach effective problem solutions in a mutual, rational, and nonaggressive way. As you will see, this chapter will help the two (or more) of you combine efforts to "defeat the problem" and not each other.

One especially sound method for reaching problem solutions, and an effective alternative to aggression, is negotiation. Chapter 6 deals in depth with this topic, teaching you in a step-by-step manner how to prepare for and engage in successful negotiations, especially with angry and aggressive people. Special sections in this chapter dealing with persuading the other person, breaking deadlocks, and overcoming obstacles should help you become a particularly effective negotiator.

Constructive communication and skilled negotiation will very often help you and the others with whom you are dealing strike a bargain or reach a mutually agreeable problem solution. Contracting, the focus of Chapter 7, is the prime method for making such bargains and solutions last. Contracts have a long history in the business world as the means for ensuring that people actually do what they have agreed to do. They have come to be used only more recently in psychology, but their purpose in the world of human relations is the same—to help make the persons involved live up to their agreements. This chapter will explore how you can plan, draw up, and put into effect powerful behavior change contracts.

A change in behavior from aggression and toward positive alternatives is also more likely to occur when positive behaviors are rewarded by successful outcomes and aggression is not. Chapter 8, on rewards and nonaggressive punishments, is mainly directed toward parents. This chapter concentrates on how you can become skilled in the use of rewards and certain nonphysical punishments to have a positive influence on changing the behavior of your child. This is accomplished without resorting to aggressive means to do so. Several of the reward methods described will also be useful to you when dealing with aggressive adults.

It is common for a person to behave aggressively not only because aggression is too frequently rewarded by others, but also because the person actually does not know how to act in alternative, nonaggressive ways. They are skilled in aggressiveness, but unskilled in such positive alternatives as listening, expressing affection, persuading others, empathy, responding to failure, setting problem priorities, dealing with group pressure, and a host of other effective and nonaggressive ways of responding to stressful or problematic events. Chapter 9,

"Positive Skill Building," describes these and many other skill alternatives to aggression. In addition, the chapter presents a detailed proven method you can use to learn these positive skills and apply them in your daily life.

Our final chapter, "Assertiveness," also presents a skill alternative to aggression, and how to learn it. We share the view with other psychologists that assertiveness is the appropriate alternative to either the extreme of aggression or the equally inappropriate extreme of passivity. We hope you can learn from this chapter to stick up for your own rights in a fair, firm, and direct manner (*i.e.,* assertiveness) without infringing on the rights of others by being aggressive and without denying your own rights by being passive.

As you can see, the contents and order of the chapters first helps you and the other person prepare to communicate constructively by calming down. Constructive communication and negotiation can then follow. Contracting and the effective use of rewards and punishments come next, as ways of making sure the solutions you have communicated and negotiated become enduring solutions. Finally, because so many of us are actually somewhat unskilled in the alternatives to aggression, we have described such skills, and how to learn them, in detail. The title, substance, and spirit of this book is *Aggress-Less.* We wish you well in your efforts to reach this most worthwhile goal.

chapter two

Relaxation

Think about the last time you got angry or frustrated. What did you do? Yelled? Cursed? Felt like hitting? Perhaps you threw something or broke something or struck someone. Regardless of what you actually did, chances are you felt tense, wound-up, or nervous. People often use the term "tied up in knots" to describe their feelings in these situations. Often, aggressive behavior is a way of releasing such tension, of "getting it out" of us. Afterwards, we may feel badly or sorry for our actions. We may have hurt someone we really care about or broken a favorite item, but we may also feel more relaxed, less tense. If only we could reduce the tension and relax in some other way, we might aggress less.

Fortunately, there are many better ways to reduce the tension. These methods are effective and easy to learn, but best of all, you can teach them to yourself. Once you have acquired these relaxation skills, you will have a tool that you can use to control the tension in any area of your life, at work or at home. As a result, you will be able to reduce the anger that so often blows up into aggression.

There are many proven methods of self-relaxation and you probably use some of them without even realizing it. For example, think of the last time you had to make a speech in public, read a paper in class, or go for a job interview. What did you do? If you're like most people, you probably closed your eyes, took a deep breath and exhaled slowly and forcefully. Maybe you gave yourself a pep talk, told yourself to relax, imagined you were somewhere else, or tried to convince yourself that this was not really so important. Ball players frequently do exercises in the on-deck circle or on the sidelines to loosen-up and you may do the same. Actually, these are all effective methods of relaxation. As we explain the various relaxation training exercises in this chapter, you will recognize many of these elements.

Right now you may be telling yourself, "I already do these things, yet it doesn't help, so why bother learning these techniques?" Well, although people informally use many of these "tricks" to reduce tension, they do not practice them enough to be really effective, they do not apply them correctly or conscientiously, and they do not think to use these same techniques when they are angry or frustrated, instead of nervous. You must learn how to relax (the relaxation skills), you must learn when to relax (the situations that call for you to apply those skills), and you must learn how to use these skills in real-life situations (when you are actually angry and feel like you are going to aggress).

First, we'll work on developing relaxation skills. As we have said, there are many different methods of relaxation. You will have to experiment to find the one that works best for you. Two of the oldest methods of relaxation are yoga and meditation, while a relatively recent development is deep muscular relaxation. All of these methods share some common elements. They all involve (1) breathing exercises, (2) reduction in muscle tension, (3) focus on internal bodily sensations, and (4) redirection of attention.

In this chapter we will deal only with meditation and deep muscular relaxation because they are the easiest to learn and apply. If, however, you have acquired skills in yoga or have access to training in yoga, you should be aware of its usefulness for tension reduction. In short, anything that relaxes you is okay.

Both meditation and deep muscular relaxation training require several weeks of practice for you to become really skillful. Fortunately, you will be able to begin using your skills within a week or so and should notice a reduction in tension almost immediately. As with most things, however, you will improve with continued practice. We will begin with meditation, for as you will see, meditation introduces many of the techniques you will use in deep muscular relaxation.

MEDITATION

Meditation involves getting focused on your bodily sensations (feelings) as a way of blocking out the tension and commotion of the outside world.

Step 1. Set aside thirty minutes of time per day that you can devote to meditation. You should try and select a time when you can be alone and will not be interrupted. Outside noises and distractions should also be kept to a minimum. Two fifteen-minute sessions (one in the morning and one in the evening) would be ideal.

Step 2. Find a quiet comfortable place where you have privacy. Let your mate know that you don't wish to be disturbed and ask him/her to help out by keeping the kids quiet, answering the phone quickly, and so on. The place you select should have a soft comfortable chair, although some people opt for sitting on the floor or on a bed. A reclining chair would be perfect, which is what most therapists use when they teach relaxation training.

Step 3. Get comfortable. Experiment with different positions until you find the one that suits you best. The traditional yoga position (sitting cross-legged on the floor) is preferred by some people. If you use a recliner or an easy chair, move around until you find a comfortable position. Close your eyes.

Step 4. Clear your mind of outside distractions and thoughts. It will help if you focus on something within your body. Take a deep breath and try to concentrate on the air filling your lungs. In some forms of meditation, the individual concentrates on a word, a sound, or a syllable which is repeated. Some common words or sounds used are *one, calm, pause* or *omm.* If thoughts come to you, just let them roll through your mind. Do not make an effort to think about them or concentrate on them.

Step 5. Take nice, slow, deep breaths. Inhale and exhale slowly. Fill your lungs and let go of the tension when you exhale. Stay within yourself. Listen to the air coming in and going out. If you have been repeating a word or sound, time the repetitions to coincide with your breathing.

Step 6. Continue the exercise for fifteen to twenty minutes. Do *not* worry about whether you are doing it correctly or if it's working or not. If you continue to practice each day, you will find that you will progressively become more relaxed and feel less tense.

Relaxation through meditation works by reducing your overall tension level. In order to be effective, it must become a regular part of your daily schedule. If your overall level of tension is lower, little things won't bother you as much and the need to "blow off steam" will occur less frequently. You may also be able to use it as a tool when you find yourself getting angry or frustrated. Simply take a deep breath, exhale the tension, and tell yourself to relax. You will find that the daily practice sessions make it easier for your body to obey the instruction to relax.

DEEP MUSCULAR RELAXATION

Some people have no difficulty in making the meditation sessions a regular part of their daily routine but others ask, "Isn't there something I can do that doesn't take so much time, something I can use only when I need it?" Deep muscular relaxation is a very effective skill, which once learned, does not require daily practice and can help you cope effectively with tension whenever it arises. Notice we say "once it is learned." This relaxation technique will take several weeks of daily practice to master, but once mastered, will enable you to relax almost instantly whenever you need to, including whenever you feel angry, frustrated, or about to become aggressive. Deep muscular relaxation is used by psychologists all over the world to help people with a wide variety of tension-related problems. There are different variations of the technique.

Deep muscular relaxation involves both tensing and relaxing the muscles in your body. Tensing them helps you recognize what tension feels like so you can identify it and make it a cue for relaxation. Part of the problem many people encounter in reducing or eliminating their aggressive behavior is that they often do not recognize the tension build-up which frequently precedes the act of aggression. If you can catch it early, it will give you a chance to do something positive to short-circuit trouble.

First, we will describe the methods for tensing each of the muscle groups in your body. It is necessary for you to become familiar with each group and the techniques for tensing and relaxing all of the groups, before you move into the actual relaxation training exercises. The muscle groups on which you should focus follow a logical pattern, beginning with the hands, moving up the arms, to the shoulders, to the head and face, down through the chest, abdomen, thighs, legs, and out through the feet. The muscle groups, and how they feel tensed and relaxed, are easy to learn. A few dry runs of the following steps will be all you'll need.

Step 1: Learning the Muscle Groups, Tensed and Relaxed

Hands. Tension is achieved by making tight fists with both hands. You don't have to dig your fingernails into your palms, but make

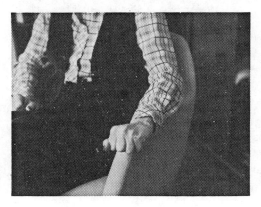

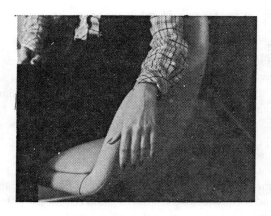

sure you can feel the tension tnroughout the hand. To relax the hands, open the fists quickly.

Arms. To tense the arms, make two tight fists again and flex your biceps, making sure to tense each of the muscles in your arm. To relax, drop your arms quickly back to the sides of the chair.

Shoulders. With your arms hanging down loosely, shrug your shoulders and try to touch your ears with them (although you can't

actually touch both ears at once). To relax, let your shoulders droop back rapidly.

Neck. Clasp your hands behind your head and press them slightly forward as you press your head back into your hands. You should feel the tension in the neck muscles. To relax, drop your hands and let your head roll gently around on your neck.

Forehead. Wrinkle your forehead by raising your eyebrows. You should feel ridges when you touch your forehead with your hand. To relax, let your eyebrows droop. The wrinkles should smooth out.

Eyes and Nose. Shut your eyes very tight (squeeze them shut) as you wrinkle up your nose. To relax these muscles, let your eyes start to open and then gently close as you release the nose muscles. Imagine your face is like putty and let the expression gently smooth out.

Mouth. Pull your lips into a tight frown. To relax, let your jaw hang open a little bit. This is important, because if you don't open your mouth a little, your jaw will remain tensed.

Chest and Back. Take a deep breath and hold it as you arch your back and put your chest out. To relax, exhale slowly as you return to the resting position.

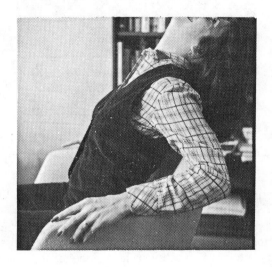

Abdomen. Tighten your stomach by bearing down and hardening the muscles, as though you were preparing to be punched in the stomach. At the same time, take a deep breath and hold it. As with the chest and back, relax by exhaling slowly as you untense the muscles.

Legs and Feet. While sitting down, lift your legs and extend them parallel to the floor as you point your toes toward your face. Tense all the leg muscles at once (thighs, knees, calves, feet). As with the previous two groups, take a deep breath and hold it during the tension phase. To relax, exhale slowly as you return to the resting position.

These are the ten basic muscle groups. Read them over several times until you are familiar with them. Practice them until you know

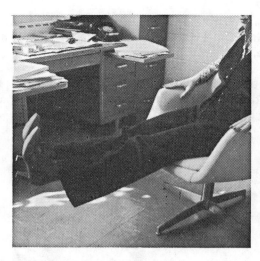

how to make each group tensed and relaxed. You are now ready to begin practicing relaxation.

Phase 1: Tension-Relaxation Cycles

Step 1. Select a time and place where you can be alone and undisturbed for about thirty minutes at a time. Again, enlist the help of your mate to watch the kids, answer the telephone, door, and so on, and keep everyone quiet. Many people prefer to practice in the evening before going to bed or just before dinner since it is easier to get privacy and quiet. Get comfortable. Put on loose-fitting clothing, take out your contact lenses or take off your glasses, and take off your shoes. The room you select should have a comfortable chair (again a reclining chair is perfect), but a sofa or bed will do. Dim the lights.

Step 2. Find a nice comfortable position, either sitting or semi-reclining. If you use a bed, put some pillows up against the headboard or wall so that you are in a semi-reclining position. Your arms should rest on the arms of the chair or if you use a bed, prop them up on pillows placed at your sides. Try different positions until you find the most comfortable one for you.

Step 3. Let your eyes close gently (do not shut them tight). You are now ready to begin. Start with the hands. Tense them (remember you do this by making tight fists with both hands) and hold the tensed position as you slowly recite "T-E-N-S-E." Say one letter every two seconds so that you are tensing the muscles for about ten seconds. You might try this first while looking at a watch so that you get a feel for the proper rate (eight to ten seconds is fine, you do not have to be exact). After approximately ten seconds of tension, relax the hands quickly and let them continue to relax while you slowly recite "R-E-L-A-X, R-E-L-A-X." Again, say one letter every two seconds so that you are relaxing for about twenty seconds. Be generous, it is better to relax longer than twenty seconds, than to relax less than twenty seconds. This is one tension-relaxation cycle. Repeat the cycle again (still with your hands). For each muscle group, you will do two cycles (Tense-Relax-Tense-Relax). Then move on to the next muscle group.

Step 4. Go through the procedure in Step 3 with each of the muscle groups outlined on pages 11–16. Remember to do two cycles with each group (Tense-Relax-Tense-Relax). Also remember that when you get to the last three groups (Chest, Abdomen, Legs), you will be taking a deep breath and holding it during the tension phase. As you do the relaxation phase for these three groups, release the breath and focus your attention on your nice even breathing.

Note: As you do each of these exercises, let your mind relax as well as your body. Like meditation, direct your attention within your body. As you tense and relax each muscle group, focus on the unpleasant feelings of tension within that particular part of your body and then on the good feelings relaxation brings to that particular part. Notice what it feels like when those muscles are tense, so that you will recognize tension when it occurs naturally. When you have gone through all ten muscle groups, you will have completed Phase 1. Phase 2 is much simpler.

Phase 2: Relaxation Only

In Phase 1 you went through two tension-relaxation cycles for each muscle group and you should now be feeling very relaxed. Think of tense muscles as stretched rubber bands. You have now relaxed those rubber bands about halfway. There is still much more relaxation to be done. In Phase 2 there is no tension, only relaxation. Beginning with your hands, concentrate on each muscle group and focus on getting them more and more deeply relaxed. Remember, do *not* tense the muscles, just *think* about letting them relax further and further. Spend about thirty seconds thinking about relaxing on each group.

Phase 3: Deep Relaxation

Finally, when you have completed Phase 2, just let your entire body relax as you focus on a pleasant scene. It sometimes helps to imagine yourself lying on the beach on a warm sunny day, or drifting peacefully on a raft in a pool, or lying under a shady tree in the cool grass on a warm day. Find an image that makes you feel good and imagine it as you relax. Let the rubber bands unwind all the way. Sink deeply into your chair or bed. Breathe deeply, slowly, evenly. Tune out the outside world as much as possible. Continue this final phase for about three minutes or so, then gradually open your eyes. You should feel refreshed and very relaxed.

SHORTENING THE EXERCISES

We have just described the complete relaxation training exercise. You should practice this once a day for about two weeks. When you feel you can relax pretty well using this complete program, try eliminating Phase 1 (the Tension-Relaxation Phase) and going right to Phase 2 (Relaxation only). Most people will be ready for this transition after about two weeks, but this is just an average. You may need more time. Don't worry about it. Relaxation will come. Simply continue with the complete program for a few more days. If, however, you find that you can relax without the complete program, then just use Phases 2 and 3 (relaxing the groups by thinking about them and relaxing the whole body at once while visualizing a pleasant scene).

After a week or so of this shortened program, you may be ready for the final step. That is, telling yourself to relax as you take a deep breath and exhale slowly, closing your eyes and imagining your peaceful scene, and trying to relax your entire body. At this point you have eliminated Phases 1 and 2 and are relaxing in response to the self-command "Relax." Once you have reached this stage you have acquired an invaluable skill, one which you will be able to use in a wide variety of situations to control anxiety, anger, frustration, and aggression.

FOCUSING ON TROUBLE SPOTS

Different people concentrate tension in different parts of their bodies. You may know some people who get stomach pains or feel nauseous when anxious, while you may know others who get chest pains or muscle-tension headaches. You may already know where you focus your tension, it may be the most difficult part of your body to relax. Extra time may be necessary for learning how to relax such body areas.

KEEPING TRACK

It is important to keep track of how well the relaxation exercises are working for you. This is easy to do and will help you to pinpoint trouble spots, areas where you have the most trouble relaxing. Imagine a scale from zero to a hundred. The zero point represents complete relaxation, no tension. Imagine the most relaxing situation you can and how it feels, then set that in your thinking as the zero point. Now imagine the most anxiety provoking situation you have ever been in (a very stressful job interview, a difficult public speech), and remember how that felt. Then set that feeling as the hundred point. You should be able to give yourself a rating between zero (relaxation) and a hundred (panic), which reflects how relaxed you feel at any time. Before you begin the relaxation exercises, rate your level of tension from zero to a hundred and record it on the "Relaxation Record" under *Before*. Do the exercises and when you have completed them, rate your level of tension again (between zero and a hundred) and record it under *After*. Finally, under *Trouble Spots* record those muscle groups that you had the most trouble relaxing.

If you are keeping up with daily practice, and are doing the exercises correctly, you should begin to notice that the *After* ratings are getting progressively lower each day (you are getting better at eliminating tension). You may also notice that the *Before* ratings are

RELAXATION RECORD

Date	Before	After	Trouble Spots

decreasing each day as well, which means that you are successfully lowering the overall level of tension in your daily life. Most importantly, you should begin to feel more relaxed.

Look for patterns in your daily notation of trouble spots. If you consistently have trouble relaxing a particular muscle group, spend more time on that group. It may mean that you focus your tension in that particular group.

RELAXATION: AN EXAMPLE

The muscular relaxation exercises we have shown you involve both tension and relaxation. We explained that one purpose of the tension exercises was to help you recognize when you are tense. Let's return to Jim and Helen Burns, our married couple.

Both Jim and Helen can sense that there is going to be trouble. Helen tells us that she sometimes knows a week in advance that tension is building up between both of them and that Jim will probably end up hitting her. Jim, too, knows that something is troubling him. Things are not going well at work, he's not sleeping well, and he notices he is beginning to lose patience with the kids and snap at Helen. Even though Jim knows something is bothering him, he doesn't know what it is or what to do about it. Jim is in the tension build-up phase that often precedes a violent outburst. This is the time to use relaxation. All of the little annoyances and frustrations tend to build up and create an elevated level of tension. By either meditating twice a day or practicing relaxation as outlined in this chapter once a day, Jim could effectively reduce that level of tension—keep it from building up. Furthermore, as things happen during the day, Jim can identify that his tension level is increasing and can use relaxation to reduce tension in each specific situation.

Suppose Jim is having a difficult week. He comes home from work after being yelled at by his boss. He has a headache and his stomach is tied up in knots. As he walks in the house the kids are fighting, Helen is screaming at them, and dinner isn't ready. Jim can feel himself about to explode in rage, but instead he takes a deep breath, exhales and relaxes himself. Although he is still not happy, he can now think more clearly about what to do next. Instead of aggressing, his mind is free to come up with a constructive alternative.

Helen could also use some relaxation as well. Remember, she is contributing to the situation by screaming at the kids. If she were more relaxed, it would also help to relax Jim. There are more effective ways of handling the children, but it helps to be relaxed in order to use them. Notice that by relaxing herself, Helen would help reduce some of Jim's tension (or the causes of his tension) and thereby would reduce the chance that Jim will aggress (and also the chance that she will aggress against the children). *Many arguments that end in violence escalate because both parties are tense.*

If either could relax, it would help to defuse the situation. Both Jim and Helen could benefit from relaxation, even if only Jim is aggressive. (Note that Helen may feel very frustrated yet not express it openly in an aggressive fashion.) Remember, at the first signs of tension, relax. The earlier you identify the signs of tension, the more effective your relaxation techniques will be.

The relaxation procedure can be summarized as follows:

The Muscle Groups
1. Hands
2. Biceps
3. Shoulders
4. Neck
5. Forehead
6. Eyes and Nose
7. Mouth
8. Chest and Back
9. Abdomen
10. Legs

Phase 1:
Tension-Relaxation Cycles

For each of the muscle groups go through two tension-relaxation cycles. Each cycle consists of eight to ten seconds of tension followed by twenty seconds of relaxation. Go through the groups in the order in which they are listed.

Phase 2: Relaxation Only

Go through the muscle groups again, but this time, just think about letting the muscles get more and more deeply relaxed. Focus on only one group at a time. Go through the groups in the same order as last time.

Phase 3: Deep Relaxation

Imagine a relaxing scene as you let your whole body relax. Breathe deeply, slowly, and regularly. Enjoy the sensations of relaxation as you spend about three minutes getting rid of the last remnants of tension.

chapter three

Self-Control

If we ask Jim Burns why he sometimes hits Helen he responds "When I get angry I just lose control." Why does Barbara Parks believe she screams and yells at her son, Tom? "I can't seem to control myself," is her response. Why do Fred Harris and Charlie Black think they fight with each other? Their arguments get "out of control" is their answer. Losing control is probably the most commonly heard excuse for aggression. Most people see it not only as the cause of their aggressive behavior but also as an acceptable reason, as if "being out of control" means they are not really responsible for what they did. When husbands beat their wives or parents hit their children, they will often apologize afterward with, "I didn't really mean it, I just lost control," as if this makes their behavior acceptable.

We do not accept the fact that people *can't* control their behavior, only that they often *don't* control it. You may feel anger, frustration, insult, or embarrassment. The other person may provoke you, hurt you, even aggress against you. But whether you respond aggressively is still your choice, and you alone are responsible for your behavior.

Taking responsibility for your behavior is an important step in controlling your aggressiveness. The phrase "don't make me spank you" as a threat used to control a child's behavior is an example of how we may try to rationalize aggressive behavior by placing the responsibility on the other person. We frequently hear abusive husbands explain their violent behavior by saying "she made me do it." We might ask, how do these people (your child or your spouse) come to have sufficient power to control your behavior? Can they make you do other things (like run through the streets naked) or just violent things? If they can make you start being aggressive, why can't they make you stop, since they probably don't enjoy being hurt? Clearly, people can't make you do anything you don't choose to do. But, why would you be reading this book if you really wanted to behave aggressively? We are not saying that you *want* to behave aggressively, only that, in reality, you *choose* to because you are *responsible* for your own behavior. There are many reasons why people choose to do things they really would rather not do. Many of this book's later chapters are devoted to teaching you what else to do. But people also do things they would prefer not to do because they have said the wrong things to themselves.

MAKING SELF-STATEMENTS

This chapter will teach you self-control, but not as a new skill which you presently lack. Rather, we will show you that already you are very much in control of what you do. It isn't as complicated as it sounds. It will become clear how much you control your own behavior if we look first at where anger comes from, since aggression most often occurs as a response to anger.

Believe it or not, people actually make themselves angry, by what they tell themselves about a situation. Let's look in on the Burns's. Jim and Helen have just gotten into bed. He feels like having sex, but she's tired, having had a tough day of work. When he suggests they have sex, she responds, "Sorry honey, I've had a tough day; I really don't feel like it tonight." Jim then thinks, "Hmm. You don't feel like it tonight; you don't feel like it any night. What about me? What about what I feel like? (getting angry) Who does she think she is? She always gets to decide whether we have sex. (getting angrier) Maybe I'm not a good enough lover for her? Maybe she's got someone she thinks is better? (enraged) She might even be having sex with someone else!"

Is it any wonder that Jim got angry with thoughts like these? Instead of these thoughts, what if Jim told himself, "Gee, she really has had a bad day. I know things didn't go well at work for her, and she has looked tired lately. She said it nicely enough, and she called me honey, so I guess nothing's wrong. Maybe she'll feel better tomorrow and we can have sex then."

In both cases the situation was the same. Helen made the same statement, and the result was the same, no sex that night. Whether or not Jim got angry was determined mostly by what he told himself about the situation. He could have made anger producing self-statements or calming self-statements, working himself up or calming himself down.

"But I don't say anything to myself, I just get angry." True, you may not actually say anything out loud, but you must be thinking these types of thoughts, otherwise you would not get angry. Psychologists call these thoughts *self-statements.* If the thoughts make us angry, we call them *negative self-statements,* while those that make us feel good are referred to as *positive self-statements.* Where do negative self-statements come from? Most of the time they come from our feelings of insecurity or worthlessness.

Let's take the example of Barbara Parks and her son, Tom. Tom's behavior is not good, as he's doing poorly in school, takes drugs, gets into trouble. While these are all undesirable behaviors that should *concern* Barbara, why do they get her angry? They get her angry because she has thoughts such as, "I can't control Tom the way a good parent should, which means I'm not very good as a parent. Where did I go wrong? Why am I such a failure? If I'm no good as a parent, I'm no good at anything." As you can see, in Barbara's thinking, Tom's behavior is seen as proof of her failure as a parent, as proof of her incompetence as a person. Is it any wonder that she gets angry at him for acting in ways that, to her, make her look so bad?

But, isn't her reasoning correct, you ask? Let's look at the situation more closely. Tom isn't a robot to be programmed, he's an independent human being. While we can have some influence on the behavior of other people, no one has actual control over someone else. Barbara could be the best mother in the world and Tom could still turn out to be a delinquent or an academic failure or a drug addict. We can only do our best to bring up our children. The rest is either luck or the influence of other people and events. While good parents have a better chance of having good children, many other things are involved: teachers, friends, relatives, strangers, and various inborn and environmental factors. Instead of using Tom's behavior as proof of her worthlessness, she would be better off telling herself positive self-statements such as, "Tom's behavior may be bad, and that doesn't make me happy, but that doesn't make me a failure as a mother. Just because he hasn't yet turned out to be the person I would like to see him become, that doesn't mean that it was my fault."

If you examine the thoughts that make you angry, you will generally find that they are of two types. We have just looked at one type, that is, when another person's behavior is proof that you are a worthless person. This may be what Jim Burns tells himself when Helen refuses to have sex with him (recall his negative self-statements that perhaps she has found a more adequate love-maker), but the Burns example also demonstrates the second common negative self-statement: That things have to be *entirely* the way we want them to be, otherwise our interaction is terrible. Sometimes we get our way, sometimes we don't. Especially when our wants involve other people, we have to recognize that they have the same rights as we do to want things their way. If Jim feels he has the right to have sex when he wants it, he also has to recognize Helen's right not to have sex when she doesn't want it. It would be nice if things could always go the way we want them to go, but it's not catastrophic if they don't (and realistically, many times, they won't).

FROM NEGATIVE TO POSITIVE

Apparently, then, we have a choice. We can tell ourselves negative things and become angry, or we can look at things in a more realistic, positive way and become less angry. How can we learn this second route, to think and say positive things to ourselves? The first step is to try and identify the negative self-statements you may be making. Whenever you find yourself starting to get angry or upset, stop and ask yourself, "What am I telling myself? How am I making myself angry?"

To practice this type of thinking, let's try an exercise. First, think about a recent experience in which you were angry. Imagine yourself experiencing the situation and the feelings again. Write down the negative self-statements you are making. Look for all such statements, but especially instances in which you're telling yourself that such and such makes you look bad or is proof that you're no good, as well as those statements that things have to be entirely the way you want them to be. Now, next to each statement write an alternative statement that disputes the negative self-statement. For example, let's say you got angry last week because your wife made something for dinner that you don't like.

Negative Self-Statements	*Positive Self-Statements*
1. "She knows I hate chicken and prepared it purposely to spite me."	1. "She knows I don't like chicken so much, so there must be a reason she made it. Maybe she was in a hurry and this was the easiest dish to make."
2. "She has no respect for my wishes."	2. "I'm not the only one in the family. I know she likes chicken and she's entitled to have what she likes as much as I am."
3. "Just because I don't make as much money as our neighbors doesn't mean I deserve to be treated like this."	3. "Before I blow this all out of proportion, why don't I try to find out why we are having chicken."
	4. "I know chicken is less expensive, and it's nice that she tries to make nice meals on our budget instead of complaining that I don't make enough money."

Notice, in this example, the husband doesn't really know why the wife has prepared chicken, but at first he just assumes the negative possibilities, while it is more likely that the positive possibilities are accurate. In the absence of the actual facts, why assume the negative, when the positive is or may be more probable. (Not to mention, less likely to lead to an aggressive response.)

Remember, when you find yourself getting upset or angry:

1. Use the anger (or upset) as your cue to start looking at what you're telling yourself.
2. Identify negative self-statements.
3. Dispute the negative self-statements by telling yourself positive alternatives.

DON'T TAKE IT PERSONALLY:
A PROBLEM-DIRECTED APPROACH

As we have seen, people often get into trouble when they take things too personally. Fred Harris tells Charlie Black that Charlie took one of his accounts and Charlie thinks the negative self-statement, "Oh. So you're saying I'm a thief." Helen Burns refuses to have sex with Jim and he thinks, "So you think I'm not a good lover." Tom Parks doesn't do something his mother asks him to do and she screams, "You never listen to anything I say, you mustn't respect me very much." In each case a statement from someone else is taken as a personal insult, and naturally people respond angrily to insults. But are these best seen as personal insults? Our answer is "No." It will be much more useful if such statements from other people are seen as problems to be solved. Let's take Fred and Charlie for instance. Fred never said Charlie was a thief. That was a negative self-statement made by Charlie. What would happen if Fred and Charlie were to look at this as a problem to be solved instead of as a personal affront?

Fred: Charlie, you took one of my accounts.
Charlie: I don't think I did, but which one do you think I took?
Fred: The bakery on Windsor Street.
Charlie: I thought Windsor Street was in my territory.
Fred: So did I.
    (Here we see a problem emerging—both Charlie and Fred think Windsor Street is in their territory.)
Charlie: Why don't we just ask Mr. Johnson to settle this one for us. *(Mr. Johnson, their boss, shows them the map and it turns out Charlie was wrong. He apologizes to Fred and hands over the sale he mistakenly made and some unpleasantness is avoided.)*

Instead of dealing with personal issues and insults, a problem is defined and a solution is arrived at. By dealing with problems instead of personalities, anger and aggression are avoided. Notice, in this example, Fred never called Charlie a thief, but what if he had? A problem-directed approach could still have been used if Charlie had remained cool.

Fred: Charlie, you're a thief, you took one of my accounts.
Charlie: *(Thinking)* I know he's upset and that's why he called me a thief, but instead of starting a fight, let's see if I can find out what's going on.

> (*Speaking in a calm voice*) Fred, I can see you're upset, but which account do you think I stole from you?

Notice here how Charlie's use of a positive, rather than negative, self-statement helped him turn his interaction with Fred into a problem to be solved rather than an insult to be responded to in kind. Once the issue is stated as a problem to be solved, both parties can help determine a mutually acceptable solution, using the constructive communication and negotiation techniques described in Chapters 5 and 6.

To summarize so far:

1. Avoid taking things personally, even when they are phrased as insults. You can do this by searching out the negative self-statements which are making you angry, and by replacing them with positive self-statements.
2. Try to see what is happening between you and the other person as a problem to be solved, rather than an insult to be taken personally.
3. Use the techniques explained later in this book to help solve the problem you have identified.

ANGER: AN IMPORTANT WARNING SIGNAL

An important part of self-control concerns knowing when you are about to become aggressive. In spite of a phrase like "she suddenly blew up," anger and aggression typically do not appear instantly. They build up slowly, often over a period of several days or even weeks. While anger can sometimes turn to aggression very quickly, usually it is a slower process. Many men who abuse their wives, and parents who abuse their children, will report that they could feel it coming. The cues are different, as some feel tense or nervous, while others report feeling frustrated. For some people, their stomachs feel knotted, they become irritable, short tempered, hot. Their neck muscles may tighten; other muscles may tense; their facial expressions, postures, rates and loudness of speech may change. They may have trouble concentrating on anything except the people or events beginning to anger them.

Think about how you get before you aggress. Try and identify those cues that signal to you that something is going to happen. Make a list of your anger cues. Study it and practice identifying the cues in your everyday relationships. Make a list in your Anger Diary (see page 32) of how you are responding to these cues. Here are a few suggestions for positive responses you can make.

1. Get out of the situation. Take a walk. Go into another room. Wash your face or have a cold drink of water. Count to ten.
2. Use your relaxation skills (see Chapter 2).
3. Identify the anger producing negative self-statements and replace them with positive self-statements as described. Don't take it personally.

THE ANGER DIARY

In this chapter we have suggested that people don't get angry automatically (and uncontrollably), but rather that they *make themselves angry* by the way they think about things. Negative self-statements and taking things personally lead to anger and aggression. Similarly, we have suggested that an effective way to control anger and aggression is by replacing those negative, self-defeating statements with more positive (less provoking) ones. We have also pointed out that it is important to "get in touch" with or recognize your early signs of anger (or aggression) and to use these warning signs as a cue that it's time to put the brakes on. In order to help you better recognize or tune in to your angry feelings, it is useful to keep an anger diary of situations and your responses.

Think of a scale from zero to ten. The zero point represents peaceful, nonaggressive feelings, while ten represents extreme feelings of anger. Whenever you feel yourself getting upset or angry, try to assign a number between zero and ten which represents how angry or upset you feel. Each day, start with a new index card. Write in headings as illustrated on the sample card (see page 32). During the day, each time you find yourself getting angry, note the situation and your anger rating before using your self-control techniques. Now use your self-control techniques and again rate your level of anger. Finally, in the results column, note what happened. For example, if you had a fight, if you spanked your child, if you avoided trouble, or if you became calm. Each evening, look at your daily card and record the number of times you feel you behaved aggressively, that is, the number of times your use

Date:			
Situation	Anger rating before using self-control procedures	Anger rating after using self-control procedures	Results
Got cut off by a driver on highway.	8	4	Yelled a little but did not chase him or challenge him to a fight.
Came home and wife told me my child had been fighting with other children.	8	3	Spoke to child with good results. No aggression.
Number of times aggressive today: _____			

Date:			
Situation	Anger rating before using self-control procedures	Anger rating after using self-control procedures	Results
Number of times aggressive today: _____			

of self-control procedures did not work and you were not successful in avoiding trouble (fights, arguments, and so on).

Each day that you are successful in avoiding angry or aggressive behavior you should arrange to reward yourself. One way to do this is to decide on something special you would really like, but would not ordinarily spend money on (for example, a new golf club, a bowling ball, book, an outfit, theatre tickets, and so on). Each day that you are successful, place a dollar in an envelope on which you have written the item you are working for. Each day that you are unsuccessful (*i.e.*, act aggressively) take out a dollar. When you have accumulated enough money in the envelope, purchase the reward for yourself. While rewarding successful self-control in this way might be an interesting and helpful means of getting started, you will soon find that your improved relationships with others (spouse, child, co-workers) is the real reward for your self-control.[1]

---

[1]What we have just described is one of many ways you can reward yourself. Later in this book (see Chapter 8), we will have more to say on this important topic, as we provide you with what you need to know to help you reward the kinds of nonaggressive behavior you are seeking.

chapter four

Calming Others

If you have learned the lessons of the last two chapters, you are now better able to relax and control your own anger, even when others are angry toward you. You are well on your way toward dealing constructively with aggression. The next step is calming the other person. He or she must also be less angry, more relaxed, more in control before positive steps can be taken by the two of you to solve the aggression-causing problem at hand. Your overall goal is to defeat the problem, not the other person. Before you can do so, before you can use improved communication, negotiation, assertiveness, interpersonal skills, or other means to deal effectively with whatever caused the aggression in the first place, *both* you and the other party must be calm. In this chapter we will describe a set of methods you can use to calm angry and aggressive people, whether or not it is you they are angry at.

MODEL CALMNESS

It is often hard to stay angry at someone who doesn't get angry back. If Helen Burns is calm while Jim is yelling, Jim is more likely to calm down. If Ben Johnson stays cool as he talks to his feuding salesmen, they too are likely to cool off. Psychologists call this imitation or contagion of a mood, *modeling*. If others around us become excited, we may also. If someone close to us models fear, we may become afraid also. If someone responds to our aggression by remaining calm, we are likely to become calm, too. So, we urge you to try to respond to aggression with calmness. You can model calmness through your facial expression, your posture and gestures, what you say, and your tone.

Specifically, a calm person's face shows an unwrinkled forehead; eyebrows even and not drawn down or together; eyes open normally, with neither the hard stare, squinting or tensed look of anger, or the wide open eyes of surprise; nose not wrinkled or with the flared nostrils of anger; mouth with lips parted normally, not pressed together as in silent anger or pulled back as in snarling. The calm person is more likely sitting than standing; arms are relaxed or at one's sides, not crossed in front; hands are open, not in fists; legs may be crossed; movements are slow and fluid, not fast or jerky; head, neck, and shoulders are relaxed, not tense or rigid. The calm person's voice is even rather than jumpy; soft or moderate rather than loud; slow or natural deliberate sounds, rather than rapid; contains pauses; and avoids shouting, sharpness, or great unevenness. These are the signs of calmness you should try to show in order to be an effective model of calmness for other people.

ENCOURAGE TALKING

You have shown the other person, by your own behavior and appearance, that you are calm, not angry. The second step in calming the other person consists of doing things to encourage the other person to talk. That is, rather than yell, shout, scream, fume in silence or pout, help the other person start explaining *why* he or she is angry and *what* he or she hopes your combined efforts will bring about. Effective steps in encouraging others to talk include asking open-ended questions (questions beginning with *what, why,* or *how*), responding to the person with encouragement (for example, "Tell me more." "Mm-hmm."), and other methods we will have more to say about shortly (listening openly, showing understanding, giving reassurance). These methods all encourage the other person to talk *more,* as explaining the source of their aggression will help calming to occur. It will also be helpful if, as we do these things to help the other person talk more, we also take other steps to make this increased talk, calm talk.

If two people are angry at each other, such as the salesmen Fred Harris and Charlie Black, a good first calming step is to separate them and deal with each alone first. When asking open-ended or other questions, ask only one question at a time, and be as specific as possible in what you ask. Tell the other person that to be sure you are understanding them, you would like them to talk lower, slower, and more simply. Also be sure to let the other person know you appreciate his or her frankness, openness and, especially, calmness.

LISTEN OPENLY

As the other person begins to respond to the calmness you are modeling, and your encouragement to talk, you will take a further step toward calming him or her if you show you are listening openly to what he or she is saying. What does *open* listening mean?

Open listening means you are really trying hard to pay attention to what the other person is saying—and you show it. You look at the other person, nod your head when appropriate, avoid interrupting, face the other person squarely, and lean toward the other person. Listening openly also means listening carefully, with sensitivity, trying to "read between the lines" to understand most fully what the other person is saying.

SHOW UNDERSTANDING

As you continue to encourage the other person to talk, and listen openly to what he or she has to say, further calming will occur if you respond by showing you understand what he or she is telling you. Sometimes this can be done very simply, for example by saying "I see what you mean," "I can understand that," or by making similar statements.

Often, showing that you understand can be done by the type of comment psychologists call "restatement of content." This involves saying back to the other person, in your own words, the essence of what

has been said to you. Such restatement or paraphrasing can successfully let the other person know you are trying hard to stay with him or
her and what he or she is saying.

Perhaps the most effective way to communicate understanding to
another person is through concentrating more on what he or she is
feeling than the content of what he or she is saying, and then let your
understanding of his or her feelings be known. Such communication,
also called *empathy,* can be a major aid to calming angry and upset
individuals. Being skilled at the use of empathy means you first must try
very hard to put yourself in the other person's place. Ask yourself what
that person is feeling and how strongly he or she is feeling it. In trying to
understand the other person's feelings, notice not only what the person
says, but how it is said—the tone, speed and loudness of words;
breathing rate; stammering; sighing; gestures; posture; facial expressions and the other clues that can be relied on to judge the nature and
strength of emotions. When you believe your understanding of the other
person's feelings, your empathy, is accurate, it is often appropriate to
communicate it to the other person.

Here are a few examples of restatement of content and reflection
of feeling.

Other person to you: "You shouldn't have left!"
   Your restatement: "You think I was wrong to have left."
     or
   Your reflection: "You're really upset that I left."

Other person to you: "Why did they stop before the end?"
   Your restatement: "You believe they gave up too easily."
     or
   Your reflection: "You feel let down that they didn't try hard enough."

Other person to you: "Damn it, they took it and it was mine!"
   Your restatement: "You think you've been cheated."
     or
   Your reflection: "You're really steamed, and feel cheated."

REASSURE THE OTHER PERSON

People who are angry or behaving aggressively, often have not tried less
forceful solutions to the problems upsetting them. Or, if they have tried

nonaggressive tactics, such tactics haven't worked. You will frequently find it quite helpful in calming such people to reassure them that nonaggressive alternatives do exist, and that you are willing to help the other person try them out.

Reassurance can be offered in a number of ways. You can say things like, "It will be okay," "We've worked this out before," "I think we'll be able to handle this a step at a time," or "I'm really interested in solving this with you." You can remind the person of times in the past when he or she, or you both, found nonaggressive solutions to this or similar problems. Your reassuring effort should be aimed at reducing threat, arousing hope or optimism, clearing up ambiguities, and making clear *your* willingness to help solve the problem. Your reassuring words should be offered warmly and sincerely, and when appropriate, with a physical gesture of support, such as a hand on the other's shoulder. If it is not overused, and if you avoid the trap of minimizing the seriousness of real problems, reassurance can be an effective aid in your calming efforts.

HELPING SAVE FACE

When it is you that the other person is angry at, your success at encouraging talking or using empathy or being reassuring will all be threatened. The other's anger toward you decreases his or her willingness to listen openly to you, to believe you, and to feel motivated to cooperate in finding nonaggressive solutions. You must do whatever you can to close the gap between you and the other person, to increase his or her willingness to join you in trying to defeat the problem, not you.

One such step is helping the other person save face, which also helps make it easier for him or her to listen openly, think objectively and constructively, compromise, and try to find effective solutions. You can help the other person save face by making it easier for him or her to retreat or back off gracefully. Avoid audiences or cornering or humiliating the other person. Provide him or her with face-saving rationalizations if necessary. Control the pace of the other's concession-giving by not asking for too much too fast. Most of all, you should also try to compromise, and offer him or her at least some substantial parts of what is being angrily demanded. At this stage of the calming process, as was true at all other stages, it is crucial that you remain calm and self-controlled. Comments by you which are provoking, belittling, critical, threatening, or even overly impatient may wipe out your otherwise successful attempt to calm the other person.

CALMING OTHERS: AN EXAMPLE

Let's see how Helen Burns used these calming methods with her husband, Jim. A letter had arrived from Helen's parents saying they planned to visit Helen and Jim in two weeks, as part of a trip they were taking to the Eastern states. Jim exploded! "They were a pain in the neck ... had to be waited on hand and foot ... bugged the kids ... bugged me ... it was short notice. I have other plans ... they'll probably stay forever." Jim carried on and on, all at top volume, getting madder, and redder, and louder. Mad at Helen's parents for their plans, mad at Helen because they were her parents, mad at the world!

Helen held back as best she could. She tried to relax, and say calming, self-controlling things to herself. Finally, having a pretty good grip on herself, Helen decided that the best next step in trying to deal with him was to calm him down, cool him off, and try to get matters to a point where they could communicate more rationally about her parents' visit.

Helen asked their children to play outside a bit (help save face), and then went into the living room where Jim was pacing and fuming. She gently touched him on the shoulder (reassurance), and softly (modeled calmness) said, "Let's see what we can work out." (reassurance) Helen sat down (modeled calmness), looked at Jim squarely (open listening), and said, "I know their visit is very upsetting to you (show understanding), can you tell me why you feel that way?" (encourage talking)

"You're damn right I can," Jim responded quickly. "First of all, it's out and out inconsiderate of them to just announce they're coming. Not ask, just announce, And then, on such short notice. Two weeks! They didn't even ask, Will you be in town? Do you have other plans? Well, as a matter of fact I *do* have other plans. I've had to postpone that fishing trip to the lake with Terry twice already, and I'm not going to do it again. Not on your life. Not for your folks or anyone. He's your son, too, would you like to tell him the trip is off?"

Helen continued leaning toward Jim and looking at him (open listening), her face and posture relaxed (model calmness), saying "mm-hmm" now and then (encourage talking), nodding as he spoke (open listening), and said, "I can see how steamed you are about this, and how it puts you on the spot with Terry (show understanding). It really is a bind for me, too. I want things to work out for your trip with Terry, but my folks haven't seen us and the kids for almost a year."

"Did you invite them?" shouted Jim. "Damn it, is that why they said they were coming then?"

"No Jim, I didn't invite them," said Helen in a moderate, deliberate voice (model calmness). "Then it's just their old selfishness again," retorted Jim, "they do what they want when they want to do it. They did this to your brother Frank, and they did it to us before, two years ago."

"Jim, I know you feel that they just keep doing this (show understanding), and you're right that they did this to us two years ago. But we worked it out then (reassurance), and maybe we can find some compromise now (help save face). What do you think?" (encourage talking).

"Well, I don't know. I just don't know. What did we do two years ago, do you remember?"

"I think we let them know we'd be glad to see them, but not the week they said," Helen replied. "Maybe we can do that again (help save face), I'd be willing to call them and suggest they see us on their return through this state instead of on the way out. How about that?" (encourage talking)

"Okay," Jim responded. "That just might work out."

In this chapter we have shown you how you can successfully calm down other people who are behaving aggressively. Try to model calmness in your own behavior, encourage the other person to talk, listen openly to what he or she has to say, show the other person that you understand what he or she means, reassure when necessary, and help save face. This combination of techniques is quite likely to work and enable you to get on with constructive, problem-solving communication.

chapter five

Constructive Communication

What has been discussed up to now is the getting ready or preparatory steps you can take when aggressive behavior must be dealt with. Relaxing, controlling yourself, and calming the other person all set the stage for dealing directly and effectively with the causes of the other person's anger, and the aggressive behavior itself. We believe that aggression between adults, or between an adult and a youngster, is best approached by honest and open problem-solving communication between all involved. You can resolve the anger, reduce the aggression, and minimize the chances they will occur again if you successfully communicate. Communication can focus on the problems or issues causing the aggression; misunderstandings between both of you; your own and the other person's perceptions and feelings; and especially on the alternative, nonaggressive ways you can deal with the problem situation. This chapter will describe and illustrate the steps you can take to be an effective communicator, even under the stressful pressure of aggressive events.

YOUR GOAL

Assume for a moment that you are about to have a serious argument with your spouse, your child, or a co-worker. One of the most important factors in determining the outcome of the argument is how you want it to come out. Is your goal to win, to beat the other person, to cut him down, to humiliate her? Remember, your intentions are crucial. If they are to defeat the other person, if it is you *versus* them, it is going to be quite difficult to either reduce the level of anger and aggression, or solve the aggression-causing problem constructively. If, however, your goal is to join with (not against) the other person in order to defeat the problem, and not the other person, your argument is off to a very positive start.

What is meant by *defeat the problem, and not the other person*?[1] We mean that Helen Burns' goal in communicating with her husband, Jim, was not to force him into accepting his in-laws' visit on their terms. Instead, it was to meet *both* Jim's needs to not have them visit then and her own needs to have them visit sometime soon. In Helen's eyes, the problem to be defeated was not Jim but, instead, how to arrange for a visit from her parents in the near future at a time acceptable to both Jim and her parents. Defeating the problem, not the other person is a *win-win* communication strategy. The people involved consider *both* their own needs and the other person's, and try to join with (not against) the other person to find a shared problem solution satisfying to both of them.

This is in clear contrast to entering an argument with a *win-lose* goal in mind. In this situation, you consider only your own needs, you seek to force the other person to see matters your way. Your goal is an outcome in which you win and he or she loses. We strongly advise against this strategy. Setting a win-win goal is much more likely than a win-lose strategy to lead to reduced aggression and lasting problem solutions.

[1]We are indebted to Alan Filley for describing constructive problem solving in this manner in his book, *Interpersonal Conflict Resolution* (Glenview, Ill: Scott, Foresman & Company, 1975), pp. 25–30.

PREPARATION

In addition to deciding on your communication goal, there are a number of steps you can take before communicating with an angry or aggressive person, which will increase your chances of problem-solving success. Some we discussed earlier, relaxing, controlling yourself, and calming the other person. Beyond these, we also urge you to:

Plan on dealing with one problem at a time. Dealing with aggression, especially when it is directed toward you, at the same time that you try to communicate constructively and also follow a win-win strategy can be a complex task. To make matters even more complex by trying to settle more than one problem at a time can be very difficult, and increase your chances of failure. So try to focus on one problem, issue, or complaint at a time. If more than one are pressing, take them in sequence, one after the other.

Choose the right time and place. Be careful where and when you try to communicate with angry people. Audiences rarely help, and can be distractions at best, further sources of aggression at worst. So seek privacy when it is possible. Also, remember that arguing in certain places can be dangerous, such as in a moving car. Choose a time and place in which you are not likely to be interrupted (by people, telephone, TV, mealtime), and will be free to finish whatever you start.

Review your plan. Try to open your mind before opening your mouth. Consider your own views and feelings. Why do you think and feel the way you do? What outcomes do you want? How can you contribute to a win-win solution? Why is the other person so upset? What does he or she think and feel? What is the other person likely to believe is a win-win outcome? Rehearse what you may say, think of how the other person may respond, and what your next response could be. Imagine the conversation you are about to have in several different forms. In thinking about what the angry person has already told you, and what you imagine he or she may tell you, try to remember that what that person says is usually an accurate description of how he or she sees the problem. However, sometimes the problem raised is not the one the other person is actually angry about—even though he or she may not know it. Does Jim Burns' yelling about his in-laws reflect his concern about their visiting, or is he really more upset about sexual or money matters? Always ask yourself before communicating with an angry person, "What is he or she *really* angry about?"

CONSTRUCTIVE COMMUNICATING

You are now ready to actually communicate with your angry spouse, child, employee, or others. Following the constructive communication rules will greatly increase the chances that the other person's aggression will be reduced and that the two of you will be able to move rapidly toward a win-win problem solution.

1. You are human, too. Just as the other person may have given you a slanted, biased, subjective version of incidents and perceptions, you may be less than 100 percent objective as well. Try to be aware of your own possible misperceptions, and don't be reluctant to openly admit them—an awareness will help you problem solve. Such phrases as "I believe that . . ." or "It seems to me that . . . " are examples of such openness to the possibility of your own subjectivity.

2. Define yourself. Explain the reasons behind your views, your interpretation of events, and your proposed solutions. Try to be logical, step-wise, and systematic. Build your case carefully and rationally, being sure to define your ideas, if necessary, as you communicate them.

3. Make sense to the other person. Keep your listener constantly in mind as you talk, and do everything you can to make yourself fully understood. Be complete in your statements, though not long-winded. Encourage the other person to ask you questions, or check out your meanings. When possible, use the other person's language and concepts to explain your ideas. Be redundant or repeat yourself as much as necessary.

4. Focus on behavior. When you describe to the other person your view of what has happened, and what you would like to happen, concentrate on actual actions the person has taken or might take—

what was done, where it was done, when it was done, how often it was done, and how much. If you focus on the person, his or her values, beliefs, intentions, motivations or other inner, unobservable qualities, rather than on things neither of you can actually do or see, your chances of progress are reduced. This is because what can't be seen (personality, character, intentions) is much, much harder to change than what can be seen (coming in on time, picking up one's bicycle, spending less money). Also for many, the focus on behavior rather than personality is far less threatening.

5. Reciprocate. As you share your thoughts and feelings about the behavior of the other person, be sure to reciprocate. Tell what *you* are willing to do—where, when, how. Be specific and concrete. Focus on your behavior, not your intentions, motivations, or similar unobservables. Avoid vague generalizations. Be especially sure, as you describe the other person's contribution to the problem, that you also are open about your own contribution to it.

6. Be direct. Present what you have to say to the other person in a direct, straightforward, nonhostile, positive manner. Say what you think, feel, believe, and prefer. Try to avoid camouflage, editing, half-truths, or hiding what you honestly believe. Make your needs, expectations, opinions, and feelings as clear as you can.

7. Keep the pressure low. As you continue to share openly your views with the other person, and your reactions to his or her behavior, your earlier successful calming efforts may start to unravel. The other person may once again become very angry and aggressive. Again, use your techniques for calming the other person as often as necessary. The art of finding win-win solutions usually requires rational discussion and calm reflection. Such solutions do not emerge from shouting or screaming matches. So, as best you can, continue throughout your entire discussion with the other person to model calmness, encourage talking, listen openly, show understanding, offer reassurance, and help the other person save face.

These procedures will usually work to keep the pressure low and restore calm even after a flare-up. If they don't, and your attempt to communicate constructively by direct and open examination of the problem causes the other person to become very angry and aggressive, and he or she stays that way, you may have to temporarily break off communication. When this happens, declare an intermission and make plans (and even an appointment) to resume your discussion at a later, hopefully less volatile time.

8. Be empathic. As you get deeper into your problem-solving discussion with the other person, it will become more and more important for you to be empathic about the other person's feelings. As we said in our earlier look at empathy as an aid to calming angry people, your first step is to try to put yourself in the other person's place. Ask yourself what he or she is feeling, and how strongly.

Communicating to the other person your understanding of his or her feelings is a crucial step in the problem-solving process. Your communication of empathy might be at the reflection level, in which you let the other person know your understanding of his or her feelings at the same level as they were shared with you. Or it might be at the implicit level, in which you go beyond what the person actually said to you, and beyond the person's own perception of his or her feelings, to share what you think may be the deeper, underlying feelings. At either level, reflection or implicit, be tentative. Say "You seem to feel . . ." "Might it be that you're feeling . . ." "My understanding of your feelings is . . ." Your effort at being empathic, especially if you are accurate but even if you are off a bit, will help make the other person feel better understood. They will appreciate your effort, and often will respond by becoming calmer, feeling closer, and trying to be empathic in return.

9. Disclose yourself. Angry people will often share their feelings with you very openly, along with the reasons for their anger. But there will be times when this will not be true. The angry person may fuss and fume, even curse and shout, without revealing the feelings underlying his or her anger or the reasons for them (*e.g.,* jealousy, resentment, sense of inadequacy, feeling cornered, and so on). You can help the other person become more open, and thus take a major step toward a constructive problem outcome, if you openly disclose *your* feelings and the reasons for them. Self-disclosure (yours) encourages self-disclosure (his or hers). Further, appropriate and well-timed self-disclosure on your part will often lead the other person to reveal feelings with which you can then be empathic.

In being self-disclosing, there are a number of things you should remember. Do it gradually, and only as it really seems to fit the discussion you are having. Be sure that your self-disclosure is appropriate in terms of amount and in such things as its depth, intimacy, length, location, and the target to whom it is directed. Above all, the goal is to make it mutual, as an aid to helping the two of you toward a fuller understanding of one another.

10. Keep it flowing. At this point in your discussion, if all is working well, information is being exchanged, feelings are being expressed and empathized with, and self-disclosure relevant to your problem is coming from both of you. There are a number of additional constructive communication steps you may want to take to keep anger reduced, aggression controlled, and the discussion moving toward a win-win solution.

The first is *check it out.* Often the message you try to send is not the one received. You mean A, the other person hears B. So check it out. As you state your views, ask the other person if he or she understands you and what you are saying. Give the other person the same feedback opportunity as well. Tell the other person what you understand him or her to mean and see if he or she agrees. Paraphrase statements made to you, and ask if that is what he or she meant. Do this several times throughout your conversation, so that misunderstandings don't take root and grow. Also be sure to ask questions. Ask about anything you don't understand, about incomplete or unclear statements by the other person, about anything standing in the way of the problem's solution.

At this stage, and at all stages of your discussion, try to pay attention to the other person's nonverbal behavior. Gestures, posture, facial expression, skin color, breathing rate, and many other nonverbal behaviors, if you watch them carefully, can tell you a great deal about the other person's feelings (is his or her anger decreasing or is he or she about to explode?); acceptance of your views (scowls, frowns, squints or smiles, wrinklefree forehead, eyes wide open); willingness to continue listening and talking (facial and posture signs of attention, movement toward or away, open or closing off gestures); and overall progress toward the problem's solution.

Try to remain at least partly in control of the content, depth, and pace of your discussion. Don't bite off at any one time more than the two of you can both chew and digest. And finally, we all respond favorably to praise, approval, or agreement from others. As you and the other person communicate, there will very often be things said to you with which you disagree. This is inevitable in parent-child arguments, marital conflicts, family disputes, and similar events, which are central to this book. But it is also true that in almost all arguments, conflicts, or disputes the other person will say things you agree with, do things you approve of, propose things you might praise. Therefore, we urge you to try to conduct constructive communication, to respond in positive ways to statements, offers, and proposed solutions by the other person of which you approve.

11. Communication blocks. So far in this chapter we have emphasized the positive things you can do to build constructive communication between yourself and another person who is behaving aggressively. Aggression reduction and good problem solutions are more attainable when you avoid certain obstacles to good communication. It is these obstacles we wish to consider.

First, some obvious *don'ts*. There are several types of messages which, in your own anger, you may communicate and which have an effect exactly opposite that of constructive communication. These messages raise the other person's anger level, increase the chances of his or her acting aggressively, and decrease the likelihood of a win-win problem solution. To the extent you are able, therefore, avoid the use of threats, commands, interruption, sarcasm, put-downs, counter-attacks, insults, teasing, and yelling.

There are also a number of somewhat less obvious steps to avoid. They may not incite the other person as directly or as quickly, but they nevertheless will work against successful aggression reduction, communication, and problem solving. These include generalizations ("You never...", "You always..."), not responding (silence, sulking, ignoring), exaggeration (of the other's position or faults, or of your correctness), speaking for the other person, offering advice prematurely, lecturing or being too long-winded, and shifting the topic inappropriately.

Finally, there are a small number of *don'ts* we would like to single out for special attention. Using them can have especially bad effects, so we wish to highlight them here.

One is a special kind of dirty fighting some have called *kitchen-sinking*. Like the cliché about throwing in everything but the kitchen sink, this involves dredging up old arguments, digging in old wounds, searching around for special weaknesses or vulnerabilities, and throwing it all at the other person. It is a type of communication which can be especially damaging to communication and the search for constructive problem solutions. Try to focus on the present problem, not old ones, and tackle one problem at a time.

Building straw men in order to then attack them can also be very damaging. Those who argue in this destructive manner distort what the other person has said, and then react to it as if the other person really had said it, rather than its being basically an invention of their own. One particularly harmful example of building straw men is a type of playing psychologist in which one person interprets or identifies the supposedly hidden motives or underlying and unconscious meanings in what the other person has said. Then the person responds to these interpretations of their own as if they were obvious, confirmed truths uttered by the other person.

Finally, you should be especially careful to avoid the use of guilt arousal as part of your communication. Playing martyr, sighing, crying, looking hurt, and saying things which try to make the other person feel responsible for unpleasant or unhappy things which have occurred are all examples of guilt arousal attempts. They will not only harm your chances of communicating constructively, but can have a harmful, lasting effect on your relationship with the other person.

CONSTRUCTIVE COMMUNICATION: AN EXAMPLE

Earlier we described the difficulties that had become chronic between Barbara Parks and her son, Tom. He had become more and more involved in avoiding school work, taking drugs, doing what he wanted to do and to hell with everyone else. The two of them found it very hard to communicate, and when they did it was often destructive and angry, ending in shouting and accusations.

Barbara knew that a particularly important time in Tom's high school years was approaching rapidly. The end of his junior year was but a few weeks away, and most of his classmates were busily studying for final exams. Most, but not Tom. Barbara was very concerned. Two of his teachers had told her he might fail their courses if final grades didn't pick up, and she suspected he was in trouble in his other two courses as well. Yet, he hardly seemed to study. Barbara decided to try to talk with him again. One more try at helping him succeed in school, and somehow at increasing *his* desire and satisfaction in doing so. (Set win-win goal) She decided she'd talk to him this evening, in the living room, right after supper (choose right time and place). His drug use and drinking had also been on her mind, but she decided to leave those matters aside for now, and just talk over his school problems this time (deal with one problem at a time).

"How can I best say to him what I think and what I feel?" she wondered to herself. "I'd like him to learn, I'd like him to enjoy school, and I'd like him to be preparing for some work he'd really like after graduating. If he fails two or three courses, he's had it. I guess it's so hard for us to discuss this because he just doesn't see it the way I do. I know he's bored and probably frustrated. He did once sort of tell me he just saw it all as irrelevant to his life. The only positive thing he seems interested in now and then is forest stuff—woods, trees, hiking, things like that. But there's hardly anything to do with that at his high school. I guess he just wants out, and that's that. I wish he didn't get so steamed up every time I brought school up. Well, this time I'll not only let him know where my head is at, but I'll really try to tune in on his feelings. If he gets upset again, and yells or sulks, I'm really going to stay calm and cool, and keep working at the problem. Calm and cool." (Preparation review.)

Later the same evening, Barbara asks Tom, "Tom, can we talk for a few minutes please?"

"What did I do now?" asked Tom.

"Listen, Tom, I just want to speak with you about something I think is important to both of us. (Be direct.) It's not only things you've done, but my feelings about where it's going to lead you. Of course, it is only my feelings about it (acknowledge own subjectivity), but I would like to talk it over with you, okay?"

"Okay," Tom replied.

"Tom, it's the middle of May now and your finals are in a few weeks, and . . ."

Tom interrupted her, exploding with anger, "Damn it, damn it! School is dumb and boring. The teachers don't care and the work they want is stupid. They can take their finals and shove them!"

"I know that you . . ." Barbara began to say, but Tom, his face getting red, interrupted again, "Look, no matter what you say it won't matter! You're not there so you don't know what it's all about. The whole school stinks! All the kids feel that way!"

"Tom," Barbara said softly (model calmness), "I can see how really upset you are about school, and the teachers and final exams (empathy-reflection level). Don't be so sure I don't understand what you mean, there was a lot I was really upset about with my own high school. Some of it was good, but I can still remember two of my teachers who were really out of it—boring, dull, just plain dull. I failed one of those classes, I think it was American history, and almost failed the other." (self-disclosure)

"No kidding," said Tom a bit less angrily. "Look, there's nothing I really enjoy there. It's just like serving time. Do you understand?"

"You're saying you feel not only bored, but that it's almost like a prison there?" Barbara replied. (empathy-reflection level)

"That's right!" said Tom, starting to get red in the face again. "I know the damn finals are coming soon, and I know I'm in trouble in some classes, but I look at the books and think 'They're really screwing me there, to hell with them!'"

"Are you saying, Tom, that even when you try to study, you get so steamed at them that you can't concentrate?" (ask questions, focus on behavior)

"That's exactly it!" Tom responded, "Exactly! I was looking at my chemistry book yesterday. Tried to read it. But I kept thinking of Mr. Harris, my teacher, and how he has it in for the class. He doesn't really give a damn. Well, if he can say the hell with me, I can say the hell with him!"

"I really do understand what you're saying, Tom, (reassurance) and how strongly you feel about this. What do you think the answer is? (ask question) I wonder if it would pay for you to talk to Mr. Harris, and to your other teachers, too? (asks question) Especially about preparing for the finals." (focus on behavior)

"I don't know. I'll take the finals, but I guess I'll fail. Maybe I won't be put in the senior class next year. I don't like that idea, but I think it's going to happen."

"You feel sort of powerless at this point. That it's just too late to make up lost ground?" (empathy-implicit level)

"I don't know if it's really too late, if I could really get into studying. I just get so mad at the whole idea that I can't study. That's the problem."

"So you think there might be time to have a go at it, but not as long as you feel the way you do. (empathy-reflection level) I can think of a few things that might help. (reassurance) One is that I will try very hard not to nag you about all this, like I know I do sometimes. (reciprocate) Another thing has to do with this pamphlet. I got it in the mail today. It's from the State Forestry Summer Programs Department. They have an eight week work camp up in the mountains for high school seniors. It sounds like just your thing. But, look, it's just for seniors. If you want to try for it, you're going to have to pass the finals. (be direct, focus on behavior) Does what I'm saying make sense to you?" (check with other person)

"This really *does* look like something," said Tom. "Let me think this all over. It's really only chemistry and English where the problems are. Maybe I can make it . . . I don't know."

Constructive communication is not always easily accomplished even under the best of circumstances. When the persons involved are not trying hard to stay relaxed, self-controlled, and calm, good communication will be even tougher to achieve. By setting "win-win" communication goals; carefully preparing how, where, and when to begin; and especially by following as many of the eleven rules for *constructive* communication that you can, your chances of getting a useful, problem-solving dialogue going will be greatly increased.

chapter six

Negotiation

In the last chapter, we focused on ways to communicate with angry or aggressive people in order to reach win-win outcomes to conflicts between both of you. In win-win outcomes, you'll remember, both people get most of what they are seeking. No one loses a great deal. Use of constructive communication to reach win-win goals should remain your best strategy, your ideal way to try to settle interpersonal conflicts and reduce aggression. But win-win outcomes are often hard to accomplish, and in a great many instances cannot be reached. It will very often be true, in interpersonal conflict situations, that one and usually both of the people involved will have to give in on at least part of whatever they are seeking. By a process of bargaining, give and take, trading off or, as we prefer to call it, *negotiation,* compromise can be sought and reached. Win-win solutions may be best, but compromise solutions, those in which both people in the conflict gain part of what they are seeking and also lose a part, are very often the optimal outcome that can be practically expected. Compromise outcomes, we feel, are almost always better than a third and rather frequent type of possible ending to an argument or other interpersonal conflict, the win-lose outcome. Here one person is victorious and the other is the victim.

In this chapter on negotiation, we will explore compromise and how to attain it. As we have done in earlier chapters, we will spell out in concrete detail how to respond to any angry and aggressive person in ways that deal with both the aggression and the problem causing it. We will describe the steps you should follow in order to be a skilled, conflict-reducing negotiator able to reach satisfying compromise goals.

NEGOTIATOR TYPES

What kind of negotiator are you going to be? Tough? Soft? Moderate? How you approach negotiating with the other person and your negoti-ating style are very important in determining whether an aggression-reducing, satisfying compromise is reached. Some people, the tough negotiators, come on strong. They open the negotiation with hard initial offers, make small and infrequent concessions, create a battling or forcing climate, and rarely reduce aggression. Conflicts are ended not with compromise solutions, but by sometimes winning everything, sometimes losing everything. In contrast, the soft negotiators start low, make large and frequent concessions and create a climate of surrender and yielding. While their giving in may often lead to reduced aggression in the other person, it also leads to a win-lose outcome, in which the other person wins all and the soft bargainer wins little or nothing.

We are clearly recommending that you try not to be either a tough or a soft negotiator. Don't dig in, demand too much or yield too seldom; don't give in, demand too little, yield too often. Compromise should be your goal, and moderation as a negotiator should be your way of getting there. We recommend a give-and-take attitude, a willingness to bargain, and an openness to yield on some matters while holding firm on others.

GETTING READY TO NEGOTIATE

Someone is angry and behaving aggressively. It may be you, or some-one else in conflict with you—a spouse, child, friend, or co-worker. Before starting to negotiate a compromise solution to the conflict, there are a number of steps you should take.

1. Keep cool and constructive. As we have said before, the procedures recommended throughout this book work best when used together. Before negotiating, if your own anger level requires it, use the relaxation and self-control methods described in Chapters 2 and 3. If the other person's anger requires it, use the methods for calming others as described in Chapter 4. And, whatever the anger levels are, all of the constructive communication methods we have described can and should be part of effective negotiation—especially, being direct and empathic, keeping the pressure low, and avoiding communication blocks.

2. Choose your tactics and goals. Get your own priorities clear before starting to negotiate. What do you hope to accomplish and what are your specific goals? The clearer these are in your own mind, the easier it will be for you to head toward them. Remember, though, that the greater the range and number of goals or outcomes which are acceptable to you, the greater the chances you and the other person will be able to reach a compromise solution.

We have several suggestions for how you might go about choosing goals to aim for. Besides the obvious matter of choosing based on what you want or need, consider (a) what is fair, (b) your relationship with the other person, and what you would like it to be after negotiating, (c) the importance to you of whatever you are negotiating about, (d) the level of risk you are willing to run, and (e) your negotiation history (success, failure, frequency, and so on) in past conflicts with this person and other persons. All of these considerations should be taken into account when you decide upon your negotiation goals.

You must also choose negotiation tactics. Earlier, we described the too tough and too soft tactics which rarely lead to compromise, and are to be avoided. Instead, we would recommend the tactics of the moderate negotiator. This person is moderate in his or her initial offer, concession size, concession rate, and compromise goal. Later in this chapter we will describe the specific negotiating techniques which effective, moderate negotiators use.

3. Size of your goal. Don't bite off more than you and the other person can chew. In planning your negotiation, remember that the smaller the issue you are tackling, the more likely you will be to succeed. This doesn't mean tackle unimportant issues, but do try to make the goal or target of your negotiation manageable. Break large

issues into smaller, more workable ones and then negotiate them one at a time. Deal with smaller ones before taking on larger ones. Among other advantages, you are more likely to succeed this way and thus create a climate of successful negotiating. If possible, plan on starting not only with smaller matters, but with those that are easiest to compromise on. This strategy is especially valuable when anger is high and trust is low.

Think of the specific language you will use in stating your position. Be as concrete as you can. Above all, in setting goals to negotiate, and in planning on the size and scope of your position, never forget the long term. Always keep in mind the nature of the relationship you want with the other person. Don't seek to win battles in ways that lose you the war. Don't sacrifice long-term goals for short-term victories. If you use tough negotiator power moves to overwhelm the other person this time, it may mean that they won't be around for you to try it again next time. A spirit of compromise should prevail in both your behavior and attitude.

4. Where and when to negotiate. Your final step in preparing to negotiate concerns the setting. As we said earlier in connection with constructive communication, negotiation proceeds best when there is privacy and little chance of being interrupted. Avoiding the presence of others is particularly important. The existence of audiences during negotiation has been shown to increase face-saving attempts, to lengthen the negotiation, to add outside pressures, and to decrease openness and objectivity. So, whenever you can, avoid the presence of those not directly involved in the negotiations.

Try to choose a neutral site (room, apartment, office) in which to conduct the negotiation. Bargainers have been shown to be more assertive and less inclined to compromise when they are in their own surroundings. So, get out of her office or his den or their apartment and find a better place to negotiate.

If possible, try to avoid time limits. Time pressures, such as appointments elsewhere or any other reason for a fixed time to end the bargaining, have a mixed effect on the outcome of negotiations. Such pressures have been shown to increase the size and number of concessions by the people involved, and in that sense they may increase the likelihood of reaching a satisfactory compromise. But time pressures also have some less desirable effects upon negotiation. They cause a lowering of goals, an increase in demands, and an increase in bluffing and other nonconstructive communication. Taken together, these mixed effects of time pressures on negotiating behavior and outcomes lead us to recommend you seek to avoid such pressures. Take as long as both people feel is necessary to reach a satisfactory compromise.

Finally, always try to negotiate in person, never by telephone. In negotiations conducted by phone, important matters are more likely to be omitted, time pressures become greater, the person called is often less prepared than the caller to negotiate, interruptions are more likely, facial expressions and gestures are not visible, misunderstandings are more frequent, and it is easier for one of the parties to say "no" when he or she can't see the other person. All of these reasons underscore the value of making sure your negotiating is done face to face.

STEPS IN SUCCESSFUL
NEGOTIATION

In our work with people in conflict, we have found that successful negotiators often go through a five-step sequence in order to reach a mutually satisfying compromise.

1. State your position. This is your opening statement. It is determined by the goals you are aiming for, the negotiating tactics you've decided to use, and how well you've prepared yourself to negotiate. Your opening position has a very large effect on how the negotiation progresses and eventually works out. It helps create the psychological climate between you and the other person, such as trust, level of toughness and cooperativeness. So choosing a moderate opening position, in which you demand neither too much nor too little, is very important to the compromise process.

2. State your understanding of the other person's position. After presenting your viewpoint, this second negotiating step lets the other person know you are trying to understand his or her viewpoint. In a conflict situation, especially when anger levels are high, it is often difficult to be accurate about what the other person believes, wants, or is demanding. Yet, for a compromise to be worked out, really understanding the other person's position is vital. So, when the other person is having trouble understanding your position, we recommend you

make use of a technique called *role reversal.*[1] You take his or her part and try to explain, argue for, and defend the other person's position, and he or she should do the same for your position. Try to really be the other person. Both of you should switch seats and names. Try to get into the other person's skin, and have him or her reciprocate. If you both do this energetically, your empathy for and understanding of each other's position will increase substantially.

3. Ask if the other person agrees with your statement of his or her position. This step is the "checking it out" we urged you to do in our discussion of constructive communication. This sequence of steps is building to the final one, in which you actually propose a specific compromise. Before doing so, you must be sure you accurately understand the other person's position, and this step is your way of doing it. So, check it out.

4. Listen openly to his or her response. The emphasis in this step is on *openly*. One or both of you are angry. One or both of you are behaving aggressively. It may be easy to hear (especially if you both are shouting!), but hard to really listen. So, as you listen openly to the other person's response to your statement of their position, you should follow all the good listening rules we described in our discussion of calming others, and also (a) don't interrupt, (b) don't tune out information you don't like, (c) don't speak before thinking, (d) discourage distractions, do nothing but negotiate, and (e) try to listen as though you have to summarize to someone else what the other person has said.

5. Propose a compromise. When you and the other person have gone through the first four negotiating steps enough times for you to feel there has been a sufficient exchange of information and increase in understanding each other's positions, it is time for a compromise solution to be proposed. Whether the compromise is some sort of fifty-fifty, split-the-difference proposal, or some other arrangement, it is important that it meets some of the needs and demands of *each* of you. Remember, in compromise solutions both of you win some of what you want, and both of you must lose a little also. It is often helpful if the

[1]You may want to have the other person read this book to help gain their cooperation, or at least explain to them in detail what you would like them to do with you and why.

compromise you propose is one that you would find acceptable if it were offered to you.

In proposing a compromise, you both demand and concede. Earlier, you chose your negotiating goals, set your priorities and now, through negotiation, you've gotten added information to help you adjust your goals or demands. When proposing to the other person what you want to get out of a compromise solution (these are your demands), and before you state what you are willing to give up or yield on (these are your concessions), try to (a) be direct, (b) be specific and behavioral (state exactly who you want to do what, where, when, and with whom), (c) explain the reasons for your demands, and (d) be sure you are reflecting your own priorities.

Tell the other person that if he or she will meet your demands, you will reciprocate with certain concessions. As with your demands, rank your possible concessions before proposing the compromise, and offer concessions first which are of somewhat lesser importance to you, those that rank low. Your goal should be to give away enough to satisfy the other person, but not so much that the compromise is a bad deal for you. When trust is low, you may have to make somewhat larger concessions or more frequent concessions in order to stimulate the other person to do likewise. But when you do so, don't burn your bridges behind you. Make sure your concessions are tentative and reversible so that you can pull back if, after you've done a good bit of conceding, the other person doesn't reciprocate.

You have negotiated toward a compromise, made your demands, offered concessions. When the two of you agree, the conflict can at least temporarily be considered over. But what about those times when you have proposed what you feel is your best compromise offer, and it is not accepted, and you feel there are no more concessions you can make? There are a number of steps you can take to persuade the other person toward your position.

PERSUADING THE OTHER PERSON

1. Agree, in part, with the other person's views. The more you are able to find and to highlight points of agreement between the two of you,

the more likely the other person's resistance to your viewpoint will be lowered.

2. State conclusions. Don't just give the other person the facts and hope he or she will accept your compromise. Tell the other person exactly and specifically what conclusions you believe the facts lead to.

3. Promote active listening by the other person. Encourage the other person to actively imagine or try your proposed compromise. Ask the person, "What would it be like if . . . ?" or similar imagination-encouraging questions.

4. Consider the other person's motivations. Slant your attempt to persuade the other person to fit his or her needs and goals. Respond to his or her sense of pride, need for status, feelings toward loved ones, or other needs and motivations you have learned about or suspect.

5. Argue against yourself. It will increase your credibility with the other person if you argue against an (unimportant) part of your own position. It may also impress the other person with your fairness and open-mindedness, and hopefully put the burden on him or her to yield on some of his or her own demands.

6. Reward concessions by the other person. Whenever the other person does yield on any of his or her demands, or move toward acceptance of any of yours, be sure to acknowledge, approve, or praise such conceding.

7. Minimize counterarguments. Include in your persuasive at-tempts weakened versions of the arguments with which the other person is likely to respond. This "co-opts" his or her response to some extent, and may increase the chances of acceptance of your proposed compromise.

8. Try to persuade gradually. Try to change the other person's thinking and behavior a small step at a time. When you try to shift the other person's position in too large a step all at one time, a boomerang effect may result. Instead of accepting your proposed compromise, the other person's resistance and demands may actually increase. You are likely to be a more successful negotiator if you attempt piecemeal changes in the other person's position.

9. Request delayed acceptance. Especially for those parts of your proposed compromise that you think the other person will find particu-larly hard to yield on, follow your attempt to persuade the other person

with the suggestion that he or she not decide immediately, that he or she think it over, and hopefully accept your view at a later point.

10. Be patient. People often need time to convince themselves, to move gradually to a new position. Give it to them. Let the give and take last as long as *both* of you feel you need. Compromises negotiated with patience are more likely to be lasting compromises.

Your use of these persuasion techniques will often be sufficient to bring the other person around to accepting your proposed compromise. At times, however, the level of conflict may be high enough, and the level of anger intense enough, that even these techniques are insufficient. You and the other person may be *deadlocked*.

BREAKING DEADLOCKS

There are a number of things you can do which have a reasonable chance of breaking negotiating deadlocks.

1. Increase bargaining room. This attempt to get things rolling again toward an acceptable compromise may mean lowering your goals a bit. The deadlock may end if you can add options or alternatives, change your terms or demands, concede a bit more, or increase your willingness to take risks.

2. Help the other person save face. The other person may be avoiding acceptance of your proposed compromise not because he or she actually *needs* further concessions from you, but because of fear that giving in or yielding means defeat or weakness. Often you can bring the negotiation to a successful conclusion if you can help the other person save face. This can be done by reminding the person about what *you* are conceding, by acknowledging the parts of his or her position you do agree with, and by showing you respect the other person's right to those parts of his or her views you disagree with.

3. Take a break. Good negotiated solutions come from rested negotiators. Tired negotiators are usually less rational, more likely to make mistakes, and more likely to settle on outcomes they may later regret. So, if one or both of you are fatigued and negotiating poorly, call for time out and take a break from the negotiation and from each other. Use the time to relax, to review your position and the other person's, to

consult other people who may be helpful, to analyze the implications of both of your positions and the deadlock, or to simply distract yourself with another activity for a while.

4. Bring in a mediator. We all need help sometimes, and you should not be reluctant to seek it. If you and the other person seem firmly deadlocked, and can't break free on your own, the two of you may have to find a third person to mediate your conflict. It must be someone you *both* agree on, and someone who hopefully can help you both with at least some of the following deadlock breakers: reduced irrationality and more objective thinking; clarified intentions, expected gains and likely costs; explorations of the implications of the proposed compromise, the reasons for your deadlock, and possible new solutions; help in graceful retreats; referee; protect; encourage openness; help you both stay cool; and help you both continue engaging in constructive communication. The person can be a friend, a relative, a counselor, or someone else. Many such people exist, so don't hesitate to seek one out.

OBSTACLES TO NEGOTIATION

During your attempts to reach a good compromise with the other person by negotiating, persuading, and breaking deadlocks, a number of obstacles may arise. Some may be the communication blocks we examined earlier. Others are especially likely to arise in and sabotage negotiations when the conflict is a heated one. One such obstacle is known as the *self-fulfilling prophecy.* This is an instance in which your expectation that the other person is likely to do something, causes you to behave in ways that increase the chances the person actually does behave that way. So, check yourself. If you anticipate that the other person is going to demand more, or cheat, or become physically abusive, or whatever, try to figure out how realistic your expectation is and whether you are communicating it to the other person. If you are, you may be bringing on yourself the very things you don't want to occur.

Or you may be provoking the other person in other ways. Are you challenging him or her unnecessarily, cornering and leaving little room for the other person to maneuver? Do you have a chip on your shoulder, is the other's aggression due mostly to your provocation? Are you making extreme or nonnegotiable demands? Are you sending contradictory or conflicting messages—ones that say "come close but stay away," or "that's a sufficient concession but I need still more," or "this is my final offer but I might have another one?" Are you both having trouble reaching a compromise because power, honor, self-esteem, reputation, saving face or status have become more important than the issues you've been negotiating? Especially crucial here is when giving in or conceding becomes equal to weakness. Or are you laying down other smokescreens which are negotiation obstacles, such as focusing at length on minor details, stalling, coming up with new issues as the first one gets "too close to home," getting hungry or making a phone call or going to the bathroom or avoiding confrontation in other ways?

These several obstacles, smokescreens, avoiders, or end runs all serve as blocks to successful, compromise-reaching negotiation. When your negotiations are stalled or seem to be failing, these are the issues to explore. And have the other person do the same. If you both can honestly deal with self-fulfilling prophecies, unnecessary challenging, extreme demands, contradictory messages, symbolic issues, and the various smokescreens we have described, you are well on your way back to concluding a successful negotiation.

NEGOTIATION: AN EXAMPLE

So far it was not proving to be a good solution. In fact, just the opposite was happening. Ben Johnson's two fighting salesmen were fighting more than ever. Rather than separate them further, and in the hope that they'd be mature enough to work it out between themselves if they had to, Ben did the risky thing of assigning them a secretary whose services they had to share. In a real sense, Ben hoped they'd see having half a claim on a secretary's services as a good chance to make peace and as a reward, since up to now they had to use the typing pool. But they were fighting as much as ever. Whose work came first? How many hours of Jane's time had Charlie used? Had Fred used? Whose reports had priority? And worst of all, each was beginning to pressure Jane to be his ally against the other.

As far as Ben was concerned things had gone far enough, no

matter how good they were as salesmen. On Friday, after a particularly heated argument between Charlie and Fred, Ben called Charlie into his office. He and Charlie went back a lot of years together, and he hoped he could make good sense prevail.

"Charlie," said Ben, "you and Fred are getting worse and worse, especially since Jane has gone to work for both of you. It's bad for her, bad for you guys, and bad for the rest of us. I really can't let this go on. You and Fred simply must get a handle on it. You've got to work it out. First thing Monday I want you to sit down with him and work it out."

"What I'd suggest you do is negotiate an agreement. Just like you negotiated the Benson deal last month, and the vacation to Pineville instead of the lake, with your wife. I want you to negotiate with Fred. I know you know how to do it, so do it with him."

Charlie saw that Ben was *very* serious. Ben didn't know it, but Charlie was really tired of going at it with Fred, and had on and off privately toyed with the idea of talking things out with him. Charlie told Ben he'd do it.

Before he even got home from work that day, Charlie began thinking about what he'd say to Fred on Monday (preparation for negotiation). "Ben is demanding a truce," Charlie thought, "and I wouldn't mind one myself (choose goals). If I try to push him around and get most of Jane's time (tough negotiator) the war will just continue. And if I tell him I'll just let all of his stuff come first (soft negotiator), then I'm getting shafted. The only answer is some sort of compromise. Sharing. He's got to give and take, and so do I (moderate negotiator). Damn, it makes me madder than hell to think about some of the things he's said to me! But I'm just going to have to stay cool to think straight (re-use self-control). Let's see, negotiate . . . compromise . . . hm-mmm. I better plan out just where I'd like this to end up (choose goals). I want half of Jane's time, but I also want all this fighting with Fred to end. So it better not be exactly half, or even every day. I better aim for *about* half her time on the average. Some days I may need more typing, some days less. If I get too exact, too much like punching two clocks, Fred and I'll be at it again, and Jane will probably become upset also. I don't need that! Okay, about half her time is fair (preparation for negotiation).

"There's got to be some room in this arrangement for emergencies, rush orders, special typing, and stuff like that. Well, maybe bringing that up right away would only confuse things (size of goal). I better take all this a step at a time. First, amount of sharing on the average. Then, special demands. Yeah, I'll try to get us to take that up second. It's really a tougher problem (smaller goals first). If we can work those out, the only other thing we'll have to settle is how to keep track. If he or I do it we'll be fighting again in a minute. It's certainly not Ben's job. Maybe Jane's the one. Maybe if we agree on these ground rules we can ask her to keep the time count.

"This isn't going to be easy. That guy really ticks me off. (Re-use relaxation.) I'll just have to keep reminding myself that neither of us is leaving Acme and we've got to learn to live with each other (remember long-term relationship).

"Ben really wants us to get to it on Monday. Probably has told Fred the same thing. Should be through by 10:00. Better get out of the office. Too many people and interruptions (avoid audiences). Maybe over at the coffee shop (choose neutral site). We could get a booth in the back, and they don't care how long you nurse a cup of coffee there (avoid time limits). Yeah, that's the place all right."

When Charlie got to work Monday morning, and came toward Fred's desk, he could tell two things right off just by looking at him, even before either of them spoke. First, that Ben had talked to Fred, and told him too that he'd better work it out. And second, that at that moment, about the last thing Fred wanted to do was talk to Charlie. Charlie thought, "This is going to be even tougher than I thought."

Charlie looked Fred straight in the eyes and said, "Fred, you and I have to talk. You know what I mean, don't you? Ben did speak to you?" Fred grunted a "yeah," and Charlie went on, "How about 10:00 over at the coffee shop?" Fred grunted a second "yeah," picked up some invoices from a pile on his desk, and began shuffling through them. Charlie turned away to go make his phone calls.

At 10:00 sharp, Charlie walked into the coffee shop and headed for a booth in the back. He ordered coffee and, just as it arrived so did Fred.

"Look Fred," Charlie began, "I'm not sure either of us are especially comfortable about this meeting. I know I'm not (self-disclosure). But Ben insisted, and I think it's probably a good idea. You need work from Jane, and so do I, and if we keep fighting over her no one will get anything done. I've been thinking it over and I'd like to make a suggestion (state your position). Can we simply aim for more or less a fifty-fifty arrangement? Jane would work for you about half the time and me about half the time. It seems the fairest and simplest way to settle this.

I think I know how you feel about this (state your understanding of the other person's position). You've been in the main office a long time, and I know you think you should have a secretary of your own. Is that how you see why we've been fighting over Jane's time (ask if other person agrees with your understanding of their position)?"

"Charlie," Fred said sharply, "I've kept my mouth shut to both you and Ben so far, but I've got plenty to say. Yeah, I should have a secretary of my own, but not because I've been in this office for twelve years. I need a full-time secretary, or at least a lot of Jane's time, because I need it. I'm handling more customers than you; my orders are more complex; I've got more letters to send and more files to keep track of than you do; I even get a lot more rush orders, special invoicing, and emergency calls than you do. I'm sure of it. I don't want more than half of Jane's time just because you're a pain. I want it because I need it."

Charlie paid careful attention to what Fred was saying (listen openly to the other person's response). He tried hard not to tune Fred out, interrupt him, or even swing back after his "you're a pain" comment (modeled calmness). Instead, he decided to see it through.

"Okay," Charlie responded, "I see where you're coming from. You've got your needs, and I'm sure they're real. But there are no more secretaries to go around, and there aren't going to be, and whatever you think about how much business you're doing in comparison to me, I've got plenty of work I need from a secretary also. Easily two and a half days each week. That's why I suggested a fifty-fifty split of her time. But look; I wasn't going to bring this up now, but I'm proposing sort of a flexible fifty-fifty split. When an emergency or rush order comes in, whether from your customers or mine, or anything else that *really* has to be done right away—we can bend the fifty-fifty rule a bit. What do you say?" (propose a compromise)

"Damn it, Charlie, it just isn't going to work! We fight enough for no reason. Give us more reason, and it'll be a disaster. The way things are now stinks, but if we keep sharing Jane's time—the old way or this new way—it will only get worse. I think we should go to Ben and ask him for separate secretaries."

"It might get worse," Charlie agreed (persuade other person—agree). "This idea of bending from a fifty-fifty split for special orders might be a particular disaster (persuade other person—argue against yourself). It might even make Jane a little crazy, too (persuade other person—minimize counterarguments). But, look, do me a favor and just sit back with your coffee for a few minutes. Think about what I'm suggesting. I mean, just take a minute and imagine what it would be like in an actual day if we did this and tried to make it work." (persuade other person—promote active listening)

"It's really hard to do, Charlie. I guess I'd have to say it might, just possibly might work, but what you mean by 'flexible' is not what I'd mean by it."

"Well, it sounds like you're saying that just maybe we can work it out, but that we've got more thinking and talking to do about it. (restatement of content) I think that's just great (persuade other person-reward concessions). Why don't we do this. Let's both think it over some more. How to split the time. If it would work and how to make it work. The special orders. Keeping Jane sane. What do you say? How about we get together here this time tomorrow? Okay? (Persuade other person—persuade gradually, request delayed compliance, be patient.)

"Yeah," responded Fred. "Let me sleep on it. Let's head back to the office" (breaking deadlocks—take a break).

The next day it somehow worked out that Charlie and Fred walked over to the coffee shop together. Charlie wasn't sure how it came to happen that way, but he thought it was a good sign.

"Charlie," said Fred after they'd settled in at the booth, "your idea just might work. I've been thinking on it, and it could make things worse than ever, but it also could be a good deal for both of us. I'd be willing to try it for a short time anyhow. But the way I've been thinking about it though is more specific than just your fifty-fifty idea. I mean, if you and I each took half the week, and built in the idea that if something rush came up she'd handle that first, well . . . I don't think that's specific enough. How about this idea? Let's split the whole week fifty-fifty, but every day at 3:30 Jane stops what she's working on—yours or mine—and checks with both of us about rush stuff. That way any rush stuff gets handled the same day. If we can try it that way, I'll go for it."

"Hey, that's great, Fred. Okay! Three-thirty every day she'll check with both of us, okay! (breaking deadlocks—increasing bargaining room). I'm really glad we've worked this out. I know you've got a lot of real secretarial stuff to get handled (breaking deadlocks—acknowledging other's position), but as I said, so do I. So let's give it a try. I'm really willing to help make this compromise work."

Your skill in negotiating mutually acceptable solutions to conflicts you are having with another person is likely to be very important, in solving the conflict, reducing the aggression, and keeping matters calm. In this chapter we have shown you how to prepare for *successful* negotiation, effective negotiating steps you should follow, ways to increase your persuasiveness, and how to overcome negotiating deadlocks and other obstacles to successful outcomes. Ample evidence exists that these several procedures, used in combination, will indeed result in satisfying negotiation results for the persons involved.

chapter seven

Contracting

In a case described earlier, Helen Burns succeeded in calming her angry husband, Jim, and worked out a compromise about her parents' visit. They would still visit, but at a later and more convenient date. As it became possible that their visit might be postponed, Jim's anger faded away. In a second case, Barbara Parks and her son struck a deal in which she would try to stop nagging him and he would try harder to prepare for his final exams, especially if he could then seek to get into a state forestry summer program. And Charlie Black and Fred Harris also worked out a compromise arrangement, one in which each gave up and got half the work time of the secretary they had to share.

All three of these solutions, and others like them, are fragile. They often are solutions which not only may be hard to reach, but also quick to crumble. The original conflict and its accompanying anger may boil up again; one of the parties may have second thoughts; the agreement may not work the first time it is tried, and one of those involved may not wish to risk a second try; someone may need to save face; or new conflicts or complications may enter the situation. For these reasons and many others, new compromises or win-win solutions often may not be lasting. Whatever you can do to make them more enduring, more binding, more likely to really be tried at some length before those involved decide to keep, change, or drop them, the better the outcomes will be. One such binder, designed to increase the chances that those making an agreement will actually try to carry it out, is the use of contracts.

A contract is basically an exchange agreement which spells out who is to do what, for whom, and under what circumstances. It makes expectations explicit, and enables the people involved to know the relative costs and benefits of doing something. A good, behavior-change contract consists of the following components:

1. Relevant dates. Every contract should specify the dates it begins, ends, or is to be renegotiated.

2. Behaviors targeted for change. This is the contract's goal, what you or the other person will do to meet the agreement. For Jim Burns, the contract goal might be to speak more quietly, yell less. For Tom Parks, to study more; for Barbara Parks, to nag less. And for the two salesmen, the contract goal is to require work of Jane for only half of each week. But such global goals are inefficient. There are ways of stating the behaviors to be changed in a contract which will maximize the chances that the changes will actually occur.

As much as possible, the goals or targets of a contract should be determined by the people who will have to meet them. When the parties involved actively participate in setting goals and related contract-building procedures, they are much more likely to have the commitment and motivation to see them through. They should try to work out *behavioral* goals, avoiding general targets or ambiguous planned changes. The specification of goals should make explicit what behaviors will be changed, by whom, where, when, how much, how often, and any other descriptions that lead to concrete and clear behavioral goals. General goals such as "behave better," or "control myself," or "stay out of trouble" are harder to both define or keep track of than such concrete goals as "avoid yelling for three days" or "talk quietly and slowly to my spouse" or "respond by telling my boss what I honestly believe or disagree about when he tries to bulldoze me." In setting such goals, remember to aim low at first. Contract for behaviors that are easier to change initially, and gradually work up to goals which are harder to reach.

In this book we have focused mostly on anger and aggression. The behavior targeted for change by many of you can be the aggression itself, with the goal of the contract being aggression reduction, control, or management. However, we recommend strongly that whenever possible, your goals be stated in terms of what you *will do,* not what you seek to *avoid* doing. Both reaching your goal, and being able to demonstrate to yourself and others that you have done so, will be made easier if you accentuate the positive. Better to make your goal "speak at a normal level" than "avoid yelling." "Dealing with others in a friendly manner" is a better way of stating your goal than is "staying out of fights." "Listening openly to my wife" is preferable to "not tuning her out." So, we urge you not only to be concrete, but to try to state your goals in terms of the acts you will actually perform, not avoid performing.

3. Rewards. A crucial part of every contract are the rewards that are promised if the individual changes the behaviors targeted as goals. This is the person's incentive or motivation for agreeing to the contract. It is the payoff or reinforcement. Psychologists have studied rewards and how they work in great detail, and know a lot about what you can do to increase the chances that the rewards in your contracts will actually work as strong motivation for behavior change.

Type of reward. Rewards can be objects, events, or other behaviors by you or the other person. In setting up a contract, be sure to let each person have a major say in choosing his or her own rewards. In this way you increase the other person's motivation to succeed in reaching the contract's goals. Sometimes reward selection can be done best by presenting the person with a list of rewards or a "reward menu" from which they can choose. In contracts between spouses, rewards that have been used are gifts, displays of affection, quiet conversation time, going to a movie, a special dinner or way of dressing, and many more. Teenagers have been parties to contracts specifying such rewards as increased allowances, time watching TV, staying out longer, having a party, and number or length of phone calls. And reciprocally, their parents' contracts have called for payoffs, if goals are reached, such as the teenager doing certain chores, homework, or getting up each morning with no hassle. Almost any event or object can serve as a reward if desired by the individual.

Amount of reward. The amount of reward to be spelled out in the contract should fit the difficulty of the contract's behavior-change goal. Easier goals should mean smaller rewards; difficult goals should result in promise of greater rewards. Ideally, the first time or two you use contracting to help change your own or someone else's behavior, you should set modest goals and promise smaller rewards for reaching them.

When to reward. It should be made clear in carrying out every contract that the reward is to be delivered *after* the person enacts the behavior contracted for, never before. Thus, it would be appropriate contractually to state: "If you do your English and chemistry homework now (behavior change goal), you may go out for two hours later (reward). The other way around, a reward before a behavior change, will almost always prove to be an ineffective contract (*i.e.*, "You can go out for two hours now, if you promise to do your English and chemistry homework later.")

Other reward rules. A reward should be given as soon as possible after the behavior change occurs. If the behavior change called for in the contract is difficult, reward should be contracted for and given for clear progress toward the overall goal. Finally, contracts should be drawn up to reward accomplishment, not obedience. The contract should state, "If you do X, you'll be rewarded with Y," not "If you do what I tell you to do, I will reward you with Y." The first approach of rewarding accomplishment, leads to independence, while the second, rewarding obedience, encourages dependence.

4. Penalties. Just as progress toward and accomplishment of a contract's goals should be rewarded, lack of progress or failure should be penalized. The penalty included in the contract, just like the rewards and goals, should be specific, concrete, behavioral, and, if possible, devised by the people making the contract. Penalties may take many forms. Losing routine pleasures (TV, dessert), doing unpleasant household chores, contributing money to political or other causes *opposite* to those you actually believe in, postponing or cancelling special events (trips, visits). Whatever the penalty chosen is, be sure it hurts enough so that there will be motivation to avoid it. Some penalties are what psychologists call *linear*, they even up the failure. For

example, a contract may be written so that a child loses a minute of play time for every minute he arrives late for dinner. Ten minutes late yields a penalty of ten minutes less play time. In other contracts, a geometric penalty is used—there is a doubling or tripling in the penalty of the nature of the failure. Coming to dinner ten minutes late brings a penalty of twenty or thirty minutes lost play time. Yet another type of penalty involves what has been called a *performance deposit.* At the beginning of the contract, the person puts up an amount of money or valuables and gets them back or gives them up permanently as he or she meets or fails to meet the behavior change goals of the contract. Regardless of the type of penalty used, the important thing is that, just as the reward given should fit the difficulty of the behavior changed, the penalty imposed should correspond to the nature of the failure which occurs.

5. Bonuses. It is often wise to include a bonus clause in your contracts. Bonuses are special rewards to be given if the person exceeds the behavior-change goal he or she agreed to try for, or reaches the agreed upon goal much more quickly than contracted for. Bonuses can be the same rewards contracted for already, but in greater quantity. Or bonus rewards can be different and even more special things you will do or get following exceptional change.

6. Record keeping. It will often be difficult to know whether or not the people involved in the contract have reached their behavior-change goals, and thus should be given a reward, penalty, or bonus, unless a clear record of their behavior is kept. You may have a general feeling that you are or are not moving ahead, but may not be sure. Keeping a record avoids this uncertainty. When a compromise or other conflict solution has been negotiated, and a contract drawn up to help make it work, it usually is a good idea to start keeping a record of the behavior involved a week or two *before* the contract starts. This base-line information can then be used by you as the standard or reference point by which to judge your progress after the contract has gone into effect. Different ways, all of them simple, have been used to keep such records—a tally sheet put up on a closet door, an index card carried with you, marks made on a calendar, a golf wrist counter, and so forth.

We have now described the clauses or components that make up a typical behavior-change contract—starting and ending dates, behavior change goals, rewards, penalties, bonuses, and record keeping.

In addition to these components, there are a number of steps you can take to strengthen the contracts you are a part of.

Contracts should be written. Contracts should always be in writing. It makes them seem like legal documents, and increases the sense of commitment and involvement of the people whose contract it is. Putting things in writing also decreases the chances that there will be a misunderstanding later on.

Contracts should be signed. The parties involved in the contract should sign it, as should one or two witnesses, if they are available. If appropriate, the signing should be a bit of a ceremony with some fanfare. Getting signatures in this manner will also help increase commitment to the fulfillment of the contract. Also be sure that each person who signs it gets a copy of it to keep.

Contracts should be fair. Rewards, penalties, and goals should be consistent with one another. As in business contracts, one must be careful to avoid ambiguous words or ideas, hidden clauses, double meanings, and fine print. All of the people who are involved in the contract should have an equal part in writing it. Force or coercion must be avoided, either in setting the terms of the contract or as the person tries to carry them out. Above all, you should not enter into a contract unless you fully intend to try to meet its terms.

Contracts should be public. Behavior-change contracts exist to help you and other people in conflict situations change behavior. Unlike business and other legal contracts, behavior-change contracts work best when they are not kept in a desk drawer, strong box, or bank vault. The more public they are, the more they can serve as a spur or reminder to the parties involved to meet its terms. So we recommend that you post your contract where it can be regularly and easily seen—on a door, a bedpost, a refrigerator, for example.

Contracts should be reviewed regularly. Human behavior is never static. In the volatile situation of conflict and the fragile circumstances of compromise, what was true yesterday may have changed by tomorrow. Use your record keeping to judge whether progress is being made. If the answer is no after a reasonable time, adjustment in the terms of the contract may be necessary. Or an entirely new contract may be appropriate. The behavioral goals may be too hard, the rewards may be too miserly, the penalties may be too great. Don't let this recommendation go unmet, review your contract regularly.

We have so far in this chapter explained what a contract consists of, and steps you can take to strengthen its effectiveness. Before presenting some examples of actual contracts, there remains one further topic to examine. The contracts we have described can be used in two different ways. For people in conflict situations, which contract is chosen may make a great deal of difference in whether or not the behavior-change goal is reached.

Good faith contracts. If a husband and wife, parent and child, or two office mates are in conflict, each member of the given pair may agree to a contract in which "If I do X, I'll get Y," independent of what the other person does. Both people in conflict agree to their own contract. The two contracts are *not* tied to each other. They are parallel, independent contracts. Tom Parks' contract may state that if he studies X hours, he gets Y reward. His mother's contract may state that if she avoids nagging him for A days, she gets B reward. In this parallel arrangement, Tom's increase in study behavior and Barbara's decrease in nagging are not tied together, but each are separately tied to independent rewards. For each person, the reward possible is usually an outside event or object, not a change that depends on the other person's behavior.

The important point here is that if the two contracts are tied together (as we will see below), and one goes down, they both do. For example, if they both sign a contract which states "If I do X, the other will do Y" ("If I, Tom, study more, Barbara will stop nagging," or "If I, Barbara, nag less, Tom will study more") and one fails to meet the responsibility involved, then there is no contractual reward motivating the other person to change. It makes considerable sense to us to recommend that the use of contracts, in most conflict relationships, start with these good faith or parallel contracts. When trust is low, and common fate a risky strategy, good faith contracts are the wisest choice.

Quid pro quo contracts. This is the other type of contract use we began to describe above. It is a linked-together, exchange, give and get contract in which both parties agree to a "You do X, I'll do Y" arrangement. Unlike the good faith contract, in which the rewards indicated were outside events or objects, the reward in a *quid pro quo* contract is always a reduction or change in someone else's problem behavior. A *quid pro quo* (something for something) contract between Tom and Barbara would state, "Tom will study X hours per day, and Barbara will avoid nagging Tom for a Y day period." As you can see, this is a common fate contract. If one party decides not to deliver, the contract is in trouble. All things considered, the risk of failure is greater for a *quid pro quo* contract than for a good faith contract. But a *quid pro quo* contract, when it works, results in the two people involved providing each other with rewards. This is the opposite of what happens in a conflict situation, where both parties seek to punish each other. Thus, the *quid pro quo* arrangement is indeed one to aim for. It provides exactly the relationship one should seek.

It seems that the wisest overall strategy in the use of contracts, therefore, is to begin their use with good faith contracts. This is consistent with the plan we have recommended a number of times of aiming low at first and then graduating to bigger possible risks and rewards. When you see that this first type of contract is succeeding, move on to the use of *quid pro quo* arrangements.

CONTRACTS

Contract 1. Helen Burns was pleased that she and her husband reached a compromise regarding her parents' visit, but was concerned that Jim had carried on so—yelling, shouting, threatening—on the way to reaching the compromise. They decided to draw up the following contract, a good faith contract for Jim.

BEHAVIOR-CHANGE CONTRACT

Behavior-Change Goal: To speak to Helen at a normal, conversational level whenever I speak to her at home or outside.

Reward: Buy myself the tie I've been admiring in the window of the men's shop.

Penalty: Not watch the bowl game next Saturday.

Bonus: Get the tie and take in the movie I've been wanting to see if our conversations go especially well.

Record Keeping: Record tallies on the wall calendar every time I speak to her the right way.

Beginning Date: 5/12   Ending Date: 5/19

Signature: _Jim Burns_

Contract 2. This contract, also a good faith agreement, was signed by Tom Parks after he and his mother worked out a compromise about his studying for final exams.

BEHAVIOR-CHANGE CONTRACT

Behavior-Change Goal: To spend two hours every weekday night until exam time studying for the chemistry and English finals.

Reward: Mother will avoid nagging or yelling about studying.

Penalty: Do the dishes two nights for every night I don't study.

Bonus: Visit the state forestry office for information about their summer program.

Record Keeping: Put a mark next to the date in my homework assignment book.

Beginning Date: 12/1   Ending Date: 12/17

Signature: _Tom Parks_

Witness: _John Benson_

Contract 3. The negotiations which Charlie Black and Fred Harris held led to this *quid pro quo* contract.

BEHAVIOR-CHANGE CONTRACT

It is hereby agreed that:

  A. Charlie Black will make use of his shared secretary's services only until 3:30 P.M. Mondays and Thursdays and all morning on Wednesdays if, in return, Fred Harris avoids seeking her services during these time periods.

  B. Fred Harris will make use of his shared secretary's services only until 3:30 P.M. on Tuesdays and Fridays and Wednesday afternoons until 3:30 P.M. if, in return, Charlie Black avoids seeking her services during these time periods.

  C. Every day at 3:30, the shared secretary will stop whatever task she is working on, check with Charlie Black and Fred Harris about rush work and, if any exists from either party, she will give that work priority.

Date: 5/2/80

Signatures: *Charlie Black* (Charlie Black)

  Fred Harris (Fred Harris)

  Ben Johnson (Ben Johnson, witness)

chapter eight

Rewards and Nonaggressive Punishment

In Chapter 3, "Self Control," we proposed that one of the reasons people resort to aggression is to control the behavior of others. Jim Burns wanted to make sure that Helen didn't cook chicken again, so he "got tough" with her. Fred Harris wanted to make sure Charlie Black didn't take his account, so he resorted to the use of threats. Parents want their children to be obedient and well behaved, often using aggression (yelling, spanking, threatening) to accomplish this goal. One way to reduce such aggressive behaviors is to provide alternate ways of dealing with people, which we have tried to provide you with. While some of the alternatives can be used with children, especially older children, they are more useful with adults. In this chapter, we will show you how to successfully influence the behavior of your children, without resorting to aggression. These techniques will help control aggression in two ways: (1) they are useful in reducing the aggressive behavior of overly aggressive children (*i.e.*, reducing aggression in your child), but equally important, (2) they will provide you, the parent, with an alternative, nonaggressive way of controlling your child (*i.e.*, reducing aggression in you).

Let's begin by introducing you to a family you haven't met yet, the Walkers. Cathy and Joe Walker are in their twenties. They were married young and had two children: Billy, age 8, and Max, age 4. Being young parents, Cathy and Joe often find it difficult to manage the responsibility of two young children. Although they love their children, they get quite upset when the children misbehave and, even though they don't want to, often end up spanking them. Lately, Cathy has been feeling more and more frustrated when her children misbehave and she is afraid that the spankings may be turning into beatings.

This problem is not unique to Cathy and Joe. Research has shown that most parents approve of spanking children for misbehavior, and more than 80 percent actually do spank their children on occasion. When spanking becomes severe and frequent it is a serious problem.

Why do parents aggress against their children? One possible reason is because they don't know how else to change the child's behavior. Another reason is that when Billy and Max misbehave, Cathy and Joe feel like they have failed as parents, thinking why else would we be unable to control our children. Since none of us likes to feel like a failure, we get angry at anyone who makes us feel that way and anger is often followed by aggression. Again, if Cathy and Joe had an effective way to influence the behavior of Billy and Max, then Billy and Max would be less troublesome and Cathy and Joe could feel better about their competence as parents.

Let's look at the other side of the story. Why do Billy and Max misbehave? Children want and need attention from their parents. All too often, unfortunately, when children are good, parents begin to take their behavior for granted and fail to pay attention to them. The old saying, "The squeaky wheel gets the grease," is appropriate here. Children often misbehave because it is a way to get their parents to pay attention to them. Even though this attention may be negative (in the form of yelling or spanking), for many children it is better than no attention at all. Children will often act aggressively or disobediently, just to get their parents to notice them. Children may also act aggressively because they have seen their parents do so. Although they may not realize it, when parents spank their children they are communicating the message that aggression is okay under certain circumstances. They are in fact modeling, or showing their child, aggressive behavior. Unfortunately, the message they send their children is that the circumstances under which aggression is justified are when you love someone or when the issue is important enough (since spanking is supposedly motivated by love and concern for the child and is more likely when something serious has happened, *i.e.,* the child has run out into the street).

Billy and Max misbehave or aggress: (1) in order to get attention, (2) because they have seen their parents act aggressively and are imitating the behavior of their parents, and/or (3) because their parents have not learned to influence their children's behavior effectively. Cathy and Joe aggress against their children: (1) because they don't know how else to change their behavior and (2) because they feel like failures as parents for having such misbehaved children. The techniques described in this chapter can help eliminate misbehavior and aggression in the children and thereby reduce aggression by parents.

SOME BASIC RULES
FOR USING REWARDS

What psychologists call *positive reinforcement* involves giving people rewards for behaving the way we want them to behave. A *reward* is anything that the person wants and enjoys. Each person has a different idea of what kind of thing he or she finds rewarding, but there are many things that *most* people find rewarding. Adults and older children, for example, usually will find money rewarding. In Chapter 7, "Contracting," we introduced the reward menu. The menu idea is appropriate in this chapter also, and it might help to review that section to refresh your memory. While children will usually work for treats (food), money, toys, and privileges, most children also find attention from adults to be a very powerful reward.

The laws of reinforcement indicate that any behavior which is followed by a reward will be more likely to occur again. Every time Billy helps with the dishes, he gets an extra helping of dessert. This reward makes it more likely that Billy will help with the dishes in the future. Whenever Max eats something on his dinner plate, his father exclaims, "That's my big boy. He eats everything on his plate, just like Daddy." By praising Max for this behavior, Joe increases the probability that Max will eat everything on his plate again next time. As this last example emphasizes, praise can be a very useful and powerful reinforcer.

Just as giving a reward can increase behavior, taking away a reward can decrease behavior. Billy gets an allowance of fifty cents a week. When Billy does poorly in school, his parents could take away part or all of his allowance. This would be a way of encouraging Billy to do better in school. Another way of removing rewards is by withdrawal of adult attention (*i.e.,* by ignoring the child). Max has learned that one way to get what he wants is to throw a temper tantrum. He lays on the floor and screams and his parents respond by pleading with him, yelling at him, bargaining with him, or by giving him attention in other ways. Eventually, they give in to his demands. In this way, they have reinforced his tantrum, that is, they have taught him that if he screams loud enough and long enough he will get the rewards of both their attention and his way. What would happen if they ignored his screaming? He would eventually learn that screaming is not the way to get what he wants and would stop. Unfortunately, he would probably not stop too quickly and, at first, would probably increase the length and intensity of the tantrum in order to really push his parents. It is therefore most important to remain firm and not give in, otherwise, you will just be teaching your child that by keeping up his or her undesirable behavior, he or she will eventually get what is wanted.

Thus far we have emphasized several important points. (1) You can get children to do something you want them to do by rewarding them for doing it, that is by giving them something they like after they do it. (2) You can get children to stop doing what you don't want them to do by taking away something they like, that is, by removing the reinforcement. (3) Your praise and attention as a parent can be an effective reward while ignoring (or removing attention) can be effective in eliminating unwanted behavior.

In the chapter on contracting, we pointed out that the reward (or removal of the reward) must follow the behavior immediately. It is equally important that the consequences be consistent. It will only confuse the child if he or she is rewarded for something one day and punished for it the next day. This is not as uncommon as it sounds. One of our clients recently related a little story about her child. While discussing an older relative, the parents were amused when their child commented that Aunt Carol had bad breath. They laughed and encouraged the child for this. The next day, when the child repeated the comment in front of Aunt Carol, they were less than pleased and promptly spanked the little child for the same behavior that they had only yesterday rewarded by their attention. It is not only important that you be consistent in the rewards or punishments you give, but also that others seeking to influence your child's behavior (spouse, baby sitter, teachers, relatives) all be consistent.

Another important idea when giving rewards is partial reinforcement. If every instance of a behavior is rewarded, we call it *continuous reinforcement,* but if only some instances of the behavior are rewarded we call it *partial reinforcement.* The best example of how partial reinforcement encourages behavior is the slot machine. The slot machine doesn't reward you (with a jackpot) every time you play it. It only rewards you once in a while. The key is that you never know when you will be rewarded. If the slot machine operated on a continuous reinforcement schedule (and rewarded you every time), as soon as it stopped rewarding you, you would quickly stop putting your money in. Since it works on a partial reinforcement schedule, it can keep you going for a long time without any rewards. How does this apply to your use of rewards with children? Very simply, if you reward a child for doing something some of the time (most of the time), but not all of the time for doing what you want him or her to do, then that behavior will be more likely to continue with fewer rewards. On the other hand, if you are trying to eliminate a behavior by ignoring it, you must be careful never to give in and reward the behavior (with attention) otherwise it will be less likely to go away. To increase a behavior, you don't have to reward every time, but to decrease an unwanted behavior you do have to ignore every time.

PARENT'S ATTENTION—
AN IMPORTANT REWARD

Parental attention is important for two reasons: (1) it may be the cause of unwanted behavior by the child (*i.e.,* to get attention) and (2) it can be an effective way of influencing your child's positive behaviors.

Let's look at how attention can be the cause of problems.

When Billy and Max are playing quietly, Cathy and Joe are happy because they can spend time together or do other things they want to do without being disturbed. Unfortunately, in doing these other things, they are ignoring the children. On the other hand, when Billy and Max are fighting, Cathy and Joe usually yell at them or hit them, both of which are paying attention to them. Although the interaction is a negative one, it may be the only way for their children to get parental attention. Cathy and Joe are inadvertently teaching Billy and Max that the way to get attention is to misbehave. They are rewarding misbehavior by paying attention to it.

Parental attention can be a powerful controller of child behavior, so why not use it to your advantage? The most effective way to utilize this potent reward is to give it following positive behavior. For example, when Billy and Max are playing quietly, Cathy and Joe should take the time to give them praise and attention. When they're being good, they should pour on the praise and spend time with them. Cathy and Joe could tell them specifically what they like about their children's behavior (*e.g.,* "It's so nice when you two play quietly together." "Billy, you're such a good boy for being nice to your brother." "Max is such a big boy, he doesn't cry and yell like a baby"). As a parent, you should be on the lookout for positive behaviors that you can praise and attend to. At first you might have to make more of an effort since you will be more used to attending to negative behaviors. You might also feel a little funny since praising positive behavior might be something you're not used to, but make the effort. Your reward will be a better behaved child.

What about ignoring misbehavior? Sometimes this is an especially useful technique. Attention in the form of yelling or hitting is one way that parents can inadvertently reward misbehavior, but there are other ways. One is by giving in to the child. We have already given you an example of this when we talked about Max, the child who throws tantrums. Max screams and kicks until his parents give in. His parents' attention and the giving in are the rewards for the screaming and kicking and they increase the chances that Max will have tantrums in the future to get both rewards. Another example is the child who simply whines and nags until the harried parents give in to his or her demands. When Cathy takes Max to the store, he runs around until he finds something he wants and then whines and nags his mother until she buys it in order to pacify him. But again, she has taught him that whining and nagging work. In these instances, we would recommend ignoring the child's tantrums and/or whining and nagging. Don't give in. Don't reward misbehavior. Don't show the child that these annoying tactics are effective. If you stick to it and don't give in (ever) you will begin to see these offensive behaviors decreasing. Keep in mind that they may increase at first (as the child tests you to see if you really mean business) but if you persist, these behaviors will disappear.

Another way parents can reward behavior is by verbally encouraging it either by bragging about it to others or by laughing at it. Remember Aunt Carol's bad breath? The parents rewarded this form of behavior by laughing at it. Some fathers will inadvertently encourage their sons to be aggressive by showing pride in such behavior. One father we know was yelling at his son for getting into a fight at school, for which the youngster was suspended. When he was done yelling he inquired: "Well, did you at least win the fight?" When the son replied that he did, the father responded proudly: "That's my boy." Although the father yelled at his son for fighting, he was clearly proud of the boy and the net result of this incident is that the son had learned that his father was pleased at this "manly" behavior.

Three general rules for using parental attention emerge from this discussion. (1) Praise positive behavior and give the child attention only when he/she is behaving the way you want him/her to behave. (2) Don't praise, encourage, laugh at, or show pride in negative behavior (behaviors you do not want to occur). (3) Ignore misbehavior, don't pay any attention to it. Don't give in to whining, nagging, screaming, or tantrums.

The third point deserves some additional comment. What, you may ask, do I do if the behavior I am supposed to ignore is dangerous to my child (or to someone else)? Do I ignore my children when they are beating each other up or when they are running into the street without looking? No, of course not. Ignoring should only be used when there is no danger involved in ignoring the behavior. If there is some danger we recommend using a *time-out* procedure.

TIME-OUT

Time-out is not a complicated procedure. Most parents may already be using it in some form without calling it a time-out procedure. Simply, *time-out* is a variation of "sending the child to his or her room," which has been practiced by parents for generations. Time-out is not only useful in controlling dangerous behavior, but is a very useful procedure for controlling any behaviors you want to change. In order to use time-out, a room must be available. The child's bedroom is usually most appropriate. With a younger child, a crib will often be used. To be maximally effective, the room should not contain toys, games, interesting distractions (books, TV set), or other objects and opportunities for time spent in the time-out room to be fun. The idea of time-out is time taken away from opportunities to do rewarding things. When the child is misbehaving, he or she is taken to the time-out room and required to stay there for a given period of time. The child should receive as little attention as possible while being taken to the room and should not be played with or attended to while in the room. The child should *not* be kept in the time-out room for an excessive amount of time (ten to fifteen minutes would seem reasonable, sometimes less) but should not be allowed out while still misbehaving. Additionally, he or she should not be allowed out as a result of whining, crying or nagging. The child should be told the conditions for release. "When you stop crying and promise to play quietly with your sister, you can come out."

What does "time-out" accomplish? It is a nonviolent, nonaggressive way of punishing your child. It eliminates the problem of attending to misbehavior because you do not pay attention to the child. You merely place the child in his or her room and leave. Try to be as businesslike and unemotional as possible. You are not modeling aggressive behavior either, because you do not hit the child and are not rough. To summarize, the rules of time-out, when your child is misbehaving you: (1) Explain that because he or she is doing _____, he or she will have to go to his or her room. (2) Remove as many playthings or distractions as possible from the time-out room (*i.e.,* put toys in a closet or toybox, turn off the TV set, and so on). (3) Either ask the child to go to the time-out room or place the child physically (but gently) into the room. Place the younger child in the crib. (4) State the time that he or she will have to remain and emphasize that this is the minimum time, and in order to get out he or she will have to be behaving positively. (5) Stick to your plan. Do not let the child whine, nag, scream, or otherwise coerce you into letting him or her out before the time is up. This will be easier for you to stick to if you use a reasonably short time. (6) Reinforce (praise) the child for behaving well while in the time-out room, and encourage the child to avoid the punished misbehavior as you let him or her out when the time-out period is over.

Thus far we have examined the use of parent attention (and withdrawal of parent attention) as ways of controlling your child's behavior. We feel that it is always important to praise your child for behaving well and encourage you to make a practice of it. Praise and affection for good behavior will give more lasting, positive results for both you and your child than will punishment and spanking (aggression) for misbehavior. It is also often useful to reward your child with tangible items (treats).

USING TANGIBLE REWARDS

In Chapter 7 we discussed contracts and suggested how these could be used effectively with adults and adolescents as alternatives to aggression. A similar technique is often used to change the behavior of children. Sometimes called a *token program,* this form of positive reinforcement is very effective with children and has been used extensively for many years. In order to use a token reinforcement program, you must first decide what behavior you wish to change. Although you may be tempted to try and change everything at once, this will not work so select something specific. Cathy and Joe were concerned that Billy was hitting Max too much so they chose that as their *target behavior,* the behavior they were trying to change. Next, decide on an appropriate reward. What would the child like and be willing to work for? Think small. Your child might like a baseball glove, but you can't buy him one every week. Billy liked to watch TV, so his parents decided to reward him with an extra half hour of TV viewing time as his reward for not hitting Max. In selecting the reward, make sure you don't pick something the child will get sick of (*e.g.,* the same type of candy). Decide on a fair rate of exchange. In this example, Billy must not hit Max all day in order to earn his half hour.

Take another example. Let's say Billy's parents wanted him to study more. For every fifteen minutes he studied, he could earn 1 token. A *token* is just a symbol, like a coin. It represents one unit of exchange. It can be a poker chip or a check on a chart or index card. The reward Billy wants is to go to a movie with his dad. Cathy and Joe would have to decide how many tokens he would have to earn in order to be able to go to the movie. They first decide that they do not want him to study all day (since he is only eight years old), but would like him to study for forty-five minutes a day. They make the rule that he can earn a maximum of 3 tokens per day (*i.e.*, for forty-five minutes studying). They would like him to be able to earn no more than one movie a week. Therefore, they decide on a rate of exchange of 15 tokens for one movie reward. They must be careful that they are not requiring too much for the reward (*e.g.*, making him study every day for three weeks to earn one movie), nor are they making it too easy (*e.g.*, he should not be able to earn four movies a week). The task, the reward, and the rate of exchange between them must be balanced and fair to both parties.

The rules of the program must be made clear to the child. He or she must know what must be done to earn tokens, what the reward will be, and how many tokens must be earned to get the reward. Here's how Cathy presented the program to Billy.

Cathy: Billy, we would like you to study more and we will make a deal with you. We want you to study for forty-five minutes a day. Every time you study for fifteen minutes we will make a check on this chart. (see example)

Mon.	Tues.	Wed.	Thu.	Fri.
☑☑☑	☑☑☐	☐☐☐	☐☐☐	☐☐☐

As soon as you get 15 checks, and you can save them from week to week, your father will take you to a movie the next weekend. You must study for fifteen full minutes to get a check and you can only earn 3 checks per day."

RESPONSE COST

You can give tokens, but you can also take them away. Taking away tokens for misbehavior is one example of a behavior change procedure called *response cost*. Let's look at the Walkers again. Remember, Cathy and Joe want Billy to play with Max without hitting him. Whenever Billy plays quietly with Max for thirty minutes, he earns 5 points. Every time Billy hits Max, he loses 10 points. Cathy and Joe keep track of the points Billy has earned (or lost) on a chart which they post on the refrigerator. Billy can exchange every point he has left at the end of the day for one extra minute of TV time. Whenever Cathy gives Billy points or takes them away, she explains why. For example, Cathy might say, "Billy, you have been playing very nicely and quietly with Max for thirty minutes, you get 5 points" or "Billy, you were fighting with Max, so I'm going to have to take away 10 points, but I'm sure if you play quietly you will be able to earn points next time." Notice, even when taking away points, Cathy remains calm and emphasizes that Billy can still earn points for being good in the future.

BONUS REWARDS

In all of the programs described so far, you will note that the points are given (or taken away) as soon after the behavior is performed as possible. In some cases, the points (or tokens) can be exchanged for rewards later in the same day, while in others, the points must be accumulated over a longer period (say for one week as in the studying—movie example). Some parents prefer to use a combination of immediate and future rewards. In the fighting example just discussed, Billy can buy one minute of TV time for each point (token) earned during that day. Each point could also go toward a larger reward which would take longer to earn. For example, we could modify the program so that each point could still be exchanged for one minute of TV time, but every day that Billy earned 20 points or more, he would also receive a gold star. He could also save the gold stars for better rewards (*e.g.*, 5 gold stars could be exchanged for a lunch out at McDonald's, 25 gold stars could be traded for a baseball glove, 50 gold stars might earn a bicycle, and so on). These rewards would depend on the child's preferences and the parent's ability to provide them. They need not be expensive. A trip to the park with mom or dad might be a very desirable, but not very expensive reward, as would tickets to a baseball game or going to a movie at night with either mom or dad. Try to use your attention, and natural rewards, such as a family outing or picnic as often as possible. It will not only be less costly, but will increase the amount of time you and your child are spending together. It is also more like the kinds of rewards that parents use naturally. Also, it will be easier to stop using the token program if you have been using these natural rewards.

RECORD KEEPING

It is essential that a chart be posted where the child can see it, so he or she can follow his or her progress. Points, checks, stars, and so on are recorded or placed on the chart as they are earned and they are subtracted as they are lost.[1]

Always remember to explain to the child why points are being added or subtracted. A sample chart follows.

Billy's Points — Monday	
10 A.M.	+5
3 P.M.	+5
4 P.M.	+10
5 P.M.	−10
6 P.M.	+5
Daily Total	+15

Billy's Gold Stars—for days he earns 20 pts. or more				
Mon.	Tues.	Wed.	Thurs.	Fri.
☆			☆	☆

ELIMINATING TOKENS

"Are these reward programs permanent, or can I eventually get my child to behave without rewards?" While token programs at first seem unnatural, a closer look reveals that just about everyone does whatever it is they do because of the positive rewards for doing it. People work for money, praise, self-satisfaction, and love, to name just a few of the most common rewards. Parents often ask: "Why should I have to pay my child to do what he or she should be doing anyway?" Recall that we never said you had to pay your child, literally. We started this chapter by explaining the use of parental attention to good behavior as a

[1]Stars are placed on index cards, which are saved from week to week until they are exchanged.

positive reward. The ultimate goal of any reward program is to get the child to behave in order to earn praise, parental approval, parental attention, and self-satisfaction.

We would again emphasize that before a tangible or token reward program is started, parents first try to use praise and attention as explained earlier. Unfortunately, if the parent-child relationship has not been a good one, because of excessive yelling or hitting, it is possible that the parent's praise and attention may not be seen by youngsters as too rewarding at first. In such cases, it is often useful to build up the rewarding value of the parent by using a token-type program to improve the relationship. Once behavior has started to improve, parent and child will have more pleasant interactions and will begin to like each other better. As this happens, parental praise, which is given along with tokens and rewards, will start to have more value to the child. Even if the child starts out by working for money, toys, or candy, he or she can later be rewarded with a family picnic or a half-hour baseball catch with dad. Once these naturally occurring events become rewarding, it will be possible to tell the child that you will no longer give points or tokens but that if he or she follows the rules of good behavior that you have been using during the program, at the end of the week you will all go to the beach, a ballgame, the park, a hamburger restaurant, and so on. In this way, you can fade out the token system while still maintaining good behavior. Remember, the important key is to always praise and pay attention to the child for good behavior.

SOME POINTS TO REMEMBER

1. Don't make it too easy or to hard to earn points. If the child only earns 1 point for playing nicely but loses 250 points for fighting, the first time the child fights he or she will give up because he or she is in too deep and can't possibly earn a reward, so why bother working for it. On the other hand, equally no good, if the child can earn 10 points an hour for playing quietly, but only loses 5 points for fighting, the child will feel that he or she can afford to fight a little, since the points can easily be made up. If the point levels don't seem to work at first, change them. Be flexible.

2. Explain everything clearly to the child. Make the rules of

behavior very explicit and repeat them if it seems necessary. If the rules are too vague or are forgotten, the child will not know what is expected of him or her. For example, a rule that is too vague might be stated: "Billy, you are to keep your room neat." The right way to state the same rule would be: "Billy, you must keep your room neat. This means your bed must be made every morning. Your toys must be in the toy box. You must pick up your clothes and either put them away or put them in the hamper."

3. Make the rewards and the rate of exchange very explicit. Tell the child exactly what can be earned and how many points he or she must make to get the reward. The wrong way to state this rule would be: "Billy, if you're good all day you can watch TV a little longer at night." Correctly stated, the rule would be: "Billy, if you play quietly with Max without hitting him for thirty minutes, you earn 5 points. Every thirty minutes, you can earn 5 more points. Every time you hit Max you lose 10 points. At nine o'clock at night we will add up your points. You can stay up and watch TV for one extra minute for every point you have earned."

4. Let the child be a part of setting up the system. Ask the child what kinds of rewards he or she would like. Let the child put the points up on the chart (or subtract them when he or she is bad).

5. If possible, try to use natural rewards such as extra TV time, going someplace nice with a parent (zoo, museum, park, ballgame, circus), a favorite meal, or a special dessert. Rewards like money, baseball gloves, toys, bikes, and dolls can be used, but they are less natural and more costly.

6. Finally, make sure you praise your child for good behavior. The token system is to be used as a temporary measure. Eventually, you want your child to behave in positive ways for praise and attention. As the child's behavior improves, your relationship should also improve and you will become an important reinforcer for your child.

chapter nine

Positive Skill Building

People may become aggressive for many reasons—frustration, pain, loss, teasing, competition, criticism, aggression from other people. We have come to believe that there is one other, very important reason why people become aggressive, a reason all too often overlooked. Aggression often occurs because people don't know what else to do! They are weak or lacking altogether in those skills which are alternative ways, different from aggression, of responding to frustration, pain, loss, competition, and so forth. They are deficient in responding to frustration with problem-solving skills, in dealing with pain through self-control, in using skilled responses to failure when a loss occurs, in reacting to competition with negotiation. Instead, their most frequent, most reliable, and most adequate response to these events is aggression.

In our view, therefore, at least part of the reason Jim Burns yelled

Note: The content of this chapter is drawn largely from the skill-building book by Arnold P. Goldstein, Robert P. Sprafkin, and N. Jane Gershaw, *I Know What's Wrong, But I Don't Know What To Do About It* (Englewood Cliffs, NJ: Prentice-Hall, Inc., 1979). The present authors wish to gratefully acknowledge the creative contribution of Drs. Sprafkin and Gershaw to this chapter.

and carried on so when Helen announced her parents' upcoming visit was that he really was not very skilled in what else he might do—problem solve, respond to her feelings, use persuasion, or even the simple skill of listening. Tom Parks' reaction to his school frustrations—to yell and scream at the world—might have occurred less often or not at all if he were better at concentrating, organizing, decision making, and goal setting.

The hopeful note here is that these many skills can be learned. Your use of aggression can fade because you've become skilled in other ways of responding, positive ways. In this chapter we will describe a large number of positive skills which can be substituted for aggression, and the specific procedures by which you, and others you interact with, can effectively learn these skills.

STRUCTURED LEARNING

In our own psychological research conducted during the past several years, we have been developing and testing a skill learning approach which we have called *structured learning*. We chose to call it this because it concretely teaches the user, in a structured way, the specific behavioral steps which actually make up the skills needed to success-fully deal with aggression. If you are able to learn the skill's steps, you have learned the skill. Before we describe the four learning procedures which make up structured learning, we wish to list a few skills taught successfully by this method, especially to people having difficulty with their own or someone else's aggression. The behavioral steps making up each skill are presented below the skill, in the exact order they should be carried out when you use the skill.

Behavioral Skills

Listening
1. Look at the other person.
2. Show your interest in that person's statement; *e.g.,* nod your head, use appropriate body language, and so on.
3. Ask questions on the same topic.
4. Add your thoughts and feelings on the topic.

Expressing a Compliment
1. Decide what it is about the other person you want to compliment.
2. Decide whether the other person would like to hear the compliment.
3. Choose the right time and place to express the compliment.
4. Express the compliment in a sincere and friendly manner.

Asking for Help
1. Decide what the problem is.
2. Decide if you want help with the problem.
3. Identify the people who might help you.
4. Make a choice of a helper.
5. Tell the helper about your problem.

Giving Instructions
1. Define what needs to be done and who should do it.
2. Tell the other person what you want him or her to do, and why.
3. Tell the other person exactly how to do what you want done.
4. Ask for his or her reaction.
5. Consider his or her reactions and change your direction if appropriate.

Expressing Affection
1. Decide if you have warm, caring feelings about the other person.
2. Decide whether the other person would like to know about your feelings.
3. Decide how you might best express your feelings.
4. Choose the right time and place to express your feelings.
5. Express affection in a warm and caring manner.

Expressing a Complaint
1. Define what the problem is, and who's responsible.
2. Decide how the problem might be solved.
3. Tell that person what the problem is and how it might be solved.
4. Ask for a response.
5. Show that you understand his or her feelings.
6. Come to an agreement on the steps to be taken by each of you.

Persuading Others
1. Decide on your position and what the other person's is likely to be.
2. State your position clearly, completely, and in a way that is acceptable to the other person.
3. State what you think the other person's position is.

4. Restate your position, emphasizing why it is the better of the two.
5. Suggest that the other person consider your position for a while before making a decision.

Responding to the Feelings of Others (Empathy)

1. Observe the other person's words and actions.
2. Decide what the other person might be feeling, and how strong the feelings are.
3. Decide whether it would be helpful to let the other person know you understand his or her feelings.
4. Tell the other person, in a warm and sincere manner, how you think he or she is feeling.

Following Instructions

1. Listen carefully while the instructions are being given.
2. Give your reactions to the instructions.
3. Repeat the instructions to yourself.
4. Imagine yourself following the instructions and then do it.

Responding to Persuasion

1. Listen openly to the other person's position.
2. Consider the other person's possible reasons for that position.
3. Ask the other person to explain anything you don't understand about what was said.
4. Compare the other person's position with your own, identifying the pros and cons of each.
5. Decide what to do, based on what will benefit you most in the long run.

Responding to Failure

1. Decide if you have failed.
2. Think about both the personal reasons and the circumstances that have caused you to fail.
3. Decide how you might do things differently if you tried again.
4. Decide if you want to try again.
5. If it is appropriate, try again, using your revised approach.

Responding to Contradictory Messages

1. Pay attention to those body signals that help you know you are feeling trapped or confused.
2. Observe the other person's words and actions that may have caused you to have these feelings.
3. Decide whether that person's words and actions are contradictory.

4. Decide whether it would be useful to point out the contradiction.
5. Ask the other person to explain the contradiction.

Responding to a Complaint
1. Listen openly to the complaint.
2. Ask the person to explain anything you don't understand.
3. Show that you understand the other person's thoughts and feelings.
4. Tell the other person your thoughts and feelings, accepting responsibility if appropriate.
5. Summarize the steps to be taken by each of you.

Concentrating on a Task
1. Set a realistic goal.
2. Decide on a reasonable time schedule.
3. Gather the materials you need.
4. Arrange your surroundings to minimize distraction.
5. Judge whether or not your preparation is complete and begin the task.

Preparing for a Stressful Conversation
1. Imagine yourself in the stressful situation.
2. Think about how you will feel and why you will feel that way.
3. Imagine the other person in the stressful situation. Think about how that person will feel and why he or she will feel that way.
4. Imagine yourself telling the other person what you want to say.
5. Imagine the response that that will elicit.
6. Repeat the above steps using as many approaches as you can think of.
7. Choose the best approach.

Making Decisions
1. Gather accurate information about the topic.
2. Evaluate the information in light of your goal.
3. Make a decision that is in your best interest.

Determining Responsibility
1. Decide what the problem is.
2. Consider possible causes of the problem.
3. Decide which are the most likely causes of the problem.
4. Take actions to test out which are the actual causes of the problem.

Responding to Anger
1. Listen openly to the other person's angry statement.

2. Show that you understand what the other person is feeling.
3. Ask the other person to explain anything you don't understand about what was said.
4. Show that you understand why the other person feels angry.
5. If it is appropriate, express your thoughts and feelings about the situation.

Setting a Goal

1. Decide what you would like to accomplish.
2. Decide what you would need to do to reach this goal.
3. Decide on the order in which you would do these things.
4. Judge whether you've planned realistically.
5. Set a realistic goal.

Setting Problem Priorities

1. List all the problems that are currently pressuring you.
2. Arrange this list in order, from most to least urgent problems.
3. Take steps (delegate, postpone, avoid) to temporarily decrease the urgency of all but the most pressing problem.
4. Concentrate on the most pressing problem.

Joining In

1. Decide if you want to join in an activity others are doing (think of advantages and disadvantages, be sure you want to participate and not disrupt what others are doing).
2. Decide the best way to join in (ask, apply, start a conversation, introduce yourself).
3. Choose the best time to join in (during a break in the activity, before the activity gets started).
4. Join in the activity

Dealing with Being Left Out

1. Decide if you're being left out (ignored, rejected).
2. Think about why the other people might be leaving you out of something.
3. Decide how you could deal with the problem (wait, leave, tell the other people how their behavior affects you, talk with a friend about the problem).
4. Choose the best way and do it.

Dealing with an Accusation

1. Think about what the other person has accused you of (if it is accurate, inaccurate, if it was said in a mean way or if in a constructive way).

2. Think about why the person might have accused you (have you infringed on his or her rights or property?).

3. Think about ways to answer the person's accusations (deny, explain your behavior, correct the other person's perceptions, assert, apologize, offer to make up for what happened).

4. Choose the best way and do it.

Dealing with Group Pressure

1. Think about what the other people want you to do and why (listen to other people, decide what the real meaning is, try to understand what is being said).

2. Decide what you want to do (yield, resist, delay, negotiate).

3. Decide how to tell the other people what you want to do (give reasons, talk to one person only, delay, assert).

4. Tell the group what you have decided.

Behavioral Procedures

1. Behavioral description. The first procedure of structured learning is to describe the skill you wish to learn in behavioral terms, so that it might be learned rapidly and effectively. We have done this for the twenty-five skills relevant to aggression. If you think of others you wish to learn, try to describe them to yourself behaviorally by *breaking the skill down into its steps.* You can sometimes do this by using your own imagination, sometimes by discussing the skill with others, and sometimes by carefully and closely watching someone who is actually using the skill just as you would like to. Wherever the behavioral steps of the skill you wish to learn come from, our list or your efforts, study and memorize them as your first step in learning to use the skill when you really need it.

2. Behavioral rehearsal. Structured learning requires you to actively train yourself so that effective and lasting learning may occur. You may be able to learn and use some skills simply by reading the skills' steps. But for most skills, passive reading of what to do probably won't be enough. Rehearsing the behavior is an excellent way for you to become actively involved in learning the skill.

Behavioral rehearsal also allows you to practice a skill's steps in such a manner that you gradually become more and more skillful in using it in the real-life situations in which you need it. The key here is gradualness. It is important that you be certain to practice the skill in easier situations before moving on to more difficult situations. We suggest you use the following gradual sequence to practice the behavioral steps for the skill you have selected.

In imagination. Think about the various situations in which you'd like to use the target skill. Pick one and picture yourself in that setting. Imagine where it is, when you might be there, and who is likely to be there with you. Imagine yourself going through the behavioral steps in the correct order and with no errors. Let the entire sequence unfold as smoothly as you can. Imagine not only what you would think, say, or do, but also what the other people involved might say or do in response to you.

Openly, alone. Now go through the correct behavioral-step sequence again, but this time say aloud what you might actually say and do in the real-life skill situation. Even if it feels a bit strange to do, try to make your words, expressions, gestures, and movements as real and as relevant as you can. Make it a true behavioral rehearsal. For reasons we will later discuss, in order to get feedback on your performance, we urge you to use a mirror in this step of rehearsal and, if available, a tape recorder.

Openly, with someone you trust. Let's assume your skill goal is "Expressing a Complaint," and you intend to develop this skill to a point at which you can express a justifiable complaint to, for example, a co-worker who has frequently treated you unfairly. You have practiced the behavioral steps that make up "Expressing a Complaint" both in your imagination, and aloud in front of a mirror, using a tape recorder. In the third stage of behavioral rehearsal, a second person becomes involved. This is your chance to go through the steps again, but this time do it while looking someone else in the eyes, responding to their comebacks. In this first attempt with someone else, the other person should, if possible, be a person you trust and who will cooperate. First, describe what skill you want to practice and why you would like help. Give your helper all the details you can about the real-life situation in which you eventually want to use the skill—where, when, why, and with which real-life target person. Tell him or her all about the person to whom you want to express your complaint . . . the individual's name, appearance, characteristics, and, most important, what response this target person is likely to have to you. Tell the person helping you to imitate the other person's behavior as closely as possible while you practice the skill. This is a rehearsal designed to teach you a skill for use where, when, and with whom you really need it. The more realistic the rehearsal, the better your real-life skill behavior will be. You may find it useful to repeat this rehearsal a number of times, until you feel fully comfortable using your new skill behavior.

Openly, with the real-life target person. Your final stage is to use the skill with the actual people in the actual places, where it counts. In using your newly learned skill behaviors at work, at home, in social situations, and elsewhere, gradually work up to using them with your target people. If it is easier for you, take on a co-worker before trying the skill with your boss. Try other skills out with people who are more cooperative before you deal with those who are less cooperative. Use the skill in less difficult situations before you tackle the really tough ones. Challenge yourself, but do it gradually!

3. Behavioral feedback. You have studied a skill and tried it out both alone and with one or more people. It's important now to determine how well you're doing. Are you carrying out the behavioral steps correctly? Are you doing them in the proper order? Could you do it better? Are you doing well in some situations but still having difficulty in others? Why aren't you getting the results you expected? Feedback on questions like these is crucial to your progress. With adequate feedback, you can eliminate errors and sharpen your skill performance. Without such feedback, your skill deficiency may remain unchanged. You or the other person may be resorting to aggression, not positive skills, too often and almost automatically. And, without feedback, you may never understand why a particular situation doesn't turn out the way you'd like it to.

You can provide yourself with behavioral feedback during the first two rehearsal stages ("In imagination" and "Openly, alone"). Use your mirror and tape recorder to help you judge honestly whether the words, expressions, gestures, and movements of your rehearsal actually fit the skill's behavioral steps. When you shift to rehearsing with someone you trust, ask that person the same questions: "Am I following the steps? How do I look and sound? Do I look natural and comfortable using the skill? Can you suggest anything I might improve upon?"

There is another type of important feedback your helper can give you. The behavioral steps that make up all of the skills in this chapter are designed to be effective means for solving whatever problem is involved. The goal in designing the steps for "Expressing a Complaint," for example, was not just to make you feel better (or to "get it out of your system") but to maximize the chances that the person you confront will respond to you as you wish (an apology, correcting an error he or she has made, and so on). Often the most important feedback we can get is results. Did it work? Did I accomplish my goal in using the skill behavior? You can get approximate answers to such questions during the rehearsal process by asking the person helping you to react to your skill rehearsal just the way the actual target person would react. If you've set up the rehearsal well, you've told your helper a great deal about the target person and his or her typical reactions. Having your helper try to be that person, especially in reacting to your behavior, can often provide particularly valuable feedback. In the example we have been using, if your helper feels your expression of a complaint would result in an apology, he or she should apologize. If your helper feels it would lead to countercomplaining toward you, he or she should do that. Urge your helper to provide you with whatever real-life reaction seems most likely. Only then can you evaluate your progress realistically and prepare adequately for real-life encounters.

It is, of course, the feedback from the real-life people themselves that ultimately tests how adequate and competent your skill behavior has been. If, in general (there may always be exceptions), people in your world are responding to you as you would like, you're probably using your skills effectively. If, on the other hand, many of your skill trials yield unsatisfying or ineffective results, there's an excellent chance that you need to work more on developing those skills. Be quite sure, however, when evaluating any negative feedback or results you receive, to discover what caused the negative results. Were you using your skills ineffectively? Or was it the case that the other person was unreceptive, stubborn, or lacking in skills? It's true that there will be some times when even though you've done your best, others may not respond quite as you hoped they would. In general, however, using a skill effectively will most often lead to rewarding outcomes.

4. Behavioral transfer. If you accurately identify the skills in which you are weak and apply the first three procedures of structured learning, there's an excellent chance you will learn the skills that were your goal. Yet, psychologists have shown repeatedly that a number of things can cause people to forget newly learned skills. They can usually use the skill when they first learn it but, all too often, a week or a month later the skill is gone. Sometimes skills disappear even more quickly, especially when you've rehearsed them successfully with a trusted friend but now have to try them with a stranger, your boss, or an angry spouse. In short, new skills are often fragile and, therefore, no skill training program is complete unless it includes procedures for making changes stick. In this section, which concerns transferring skill behavior from where you learned it to where you need it, we will present a number of possible ways you can minimize skill loss. Through the use of these techniques you can both increase the chances of holding on to what you've learned, and sharpen your skills even further.

Be sure your original learning of the skill is sufficient. Of the several reasons why you may forget a newly learned skill, not learning it well enough in the beginning is the easiest to correct. Usually, the main reason turns out to be not enough rehearsal or not enough feedback. You can increase the chances that your new skill will hold up over time, therefore, by (1) increasing the quantity of rehearsals before trying a skill in real-life settings and (2) finding better sources of feedback about the quality of your skill use. When you do rehearse a skill, be sure to practice several times after you've used it as well. Don't stop after only using the skill well once or twice. Keep going, even though you feel you've got it. Psychologists call this *overlearning,* and it works!

Be sure your original learning of the skill is realistic enough. Psychologists have found that the more similar the practice situation is to the actual situation, the better you'll retain the skill. That is, sometimes a skill can be learned well but in a form that makes it difficult to transfer the skill to where you need it—on the job, at home, on a date, and so on. In a case like this, you should consider such matters as (1) how realistic your original rehearsal of the skill was and (2) how many people and how many different kinds of people you originally rehearsed the skill with. You can make the learning situation more realistic by rehearsing the skill with people and in places most similar to the real-life people and places in which you need the skill. You can make the learning situation more varied by rehearsing the skill with several different people. The greater the variety of other people you practice the skill with, the greater the chances that some of these practice partners will be similar to the people with whom you'll need to use the skill in actual situations.

Instruct yourself in ways that keep your skill use effective. As became clear in our earlier discussion of self-control, psychological research supports the idea that it is often useful to talk to yourself! This self-instruction research shows the benefits of coaching yourself, prompting yourself, guiding yourself, and encouraging yourself. So, to help make your skills stick, we urge you to do the following.

1. Remind or prompt yourself sufficiently about the skill's behavioral steps when you're in a real-life situation in which you need the skill.
2. Say encouraging things to yourself—"You can do it!"—rather than dwelling on possible skill failure.
3. Note the similarities (and/or differences) between a past situation in which a skill worked well and a current situation in which you are less effective in using the skill. If there are similarities, perhaps you should use the skill in a similar manner; if there are differences, you may have to use it (the skill) differently or combine it with other skills, or perhaps not even use it at all and replace it with another skill.
4. Point out to yourself the specific benefits that you will probably accrue if you use the skill correctly, as well as the negative outcomes you're likely to avoid in this way.

Maximize the chances that others will reward you if you can use the skill correctly. If others praise, approve, agree, comply, or otherwise reward you, you're likely to keep using a skill. If they complain, disapprove, disagree, ignore, reject, or otherwise punish you, your skill behaviors are destined to fade away. Following are steps you can take to maximize the chances that your correct use of the skill will be rewarded by others.

1. Say and do things that try to change what others expect of you. Instruct them; change their anticipations about how they expect you to behave; ask them to pay attention to the new things you are doing.

2. Ask other important people in your life to change their behavior so that it is compatible with or complements or rewards the skill behaviors you're using. Ask your spouse, for example, to use the skills that seem to go along with the skills you are trying to use. For example, ask him or her to respond with "Listening" or "Responding to Your Feelings" when you "Express Affection" or "Express a Complaint." You might even ask your boss to "Negotiate" with you when you are trying to "Negotiate" with him.

3. Go places, choose times, and select people who are likely to reward your effective skill use.

4. Avoid places, times, and people that are unlikely to reward effective skill use.

Provide yourself with sufficient and appropriate self-rewards for using the skill correctly. You can also use self-rewards to help you avoid forgetting skill behaviors. Remember, rewards do not only come from others. You can and should reward yourself, both by what you say to yourself and by things you do for yourself. *Self-reward,* therefore, is a combination of saying something encouraging to yourself and doing something special for yourself. You should follow certain rules to be sure that your self-rewards have a maximum effect in helping you to retain the skills you've learned.

1. Choose your rewards carefully. Be sure that the rewarding statement you make to yourself is clear and unambiguous, *e.g.,* "I really handled that well." Be sure that the special thing you do for yourself isn't something you'd do anyhow. For example, don't reward yourself by buying something you already planned to buy. Don't go to a certain movie as a reward if you would have seen it even if you hadn't used a skill especially well. A second type of "doing for yourself" reward can be everyday things you would usually get anyway, but that you're now denying yourself until you use the skill well. For example, save that special dessert or expensive cigar as a reward that you can present yourself for good progress.

2. Always reward yourself immediately after you use the skill well, or as soon as possible after. Don't delay in self-reward if it's at all possible. The greater the delay, the greater the chances that your self-reward will fail to serve its purpose of helping to make changes stick.

3. Be very careful to reward yourself only when you have used the skill well. Saying nice things to yourself and doing nice things for yourself should occur only when you've followed all the skill's behavioral steps. When you have followed only some of them well, we suggest you provide yourself with a verbal self-reward only, *e.g.,* "Good try."

Choose which skills to use very carefully. You may learn a number of the skills described in this chapter, and chances are that when you set out to use them in actual situations you (wisely) try one skill at a time. Getting along effectively in the real world, however, often demands more. Many times, a problem can't be solved or a relationship established unless you skillfully use a combination or a sequence of skills. For example, before you can effectively use the skill "Negotiating," you may first have to be equally effective in "Setting Problem Priorities" and "Making a Decision." In general, before entering a real-life situation, it's frequently useful to consider the situation carefully. Ask yourself what skills this situation might demand of you. This type of planning for use of specific skill combinations or skill sequences can often prove to be quite valuable. There is no magic formula for figuring out which skills you'll need, or in what order you'll need them. Rather, success at planning skill sequences is usually a matter of thinking carefully about what you and the others involved in an actual situation are likely to do. Focus on the actual behavior that is likely to take place.

Work at it a bit and you'll find that even the most complex situations can be broken down into the skills that are likely to be needed. After doing this a while, there is a very good chance you'll become an expert at this type of skill-use planning.

POSITIVE SKILL BUILDING:
AN EXAMPLE

Jim and Helen Burns fought over a lot more than just occasional visits from her parents, such as their children's discipline, their tight budget, their sexual problems, and big things like their future and little things like which movie to see. One particularly frequent argument, which happened at least twice a week in the months since Helen had taken a job, had to do with sharing household chores.

Jim would come home from work and hardly ever lift a finger. Sure he was tired, but he would plop down in front of the TV, and wait for the world to wait on him. Helen would come home from her job, have to fix dinner, take care of the children, clean up the kitchen, and other household chores that needed to be done. Sometimes Helen responded with a slow burn, saying nothing, but really fuming inside. Other times she'd yell and shout as loud as Jim ever did, demanding at the top of her voice that he get off his behind and help out.

Well, she was really getting nowhere. Keeping quiet didn't work; blowing her top was no better. There had to be a middle course. There had to be a skill that she just wasn't using to fit this situation. Helen thought long and hard about the structured learning skills and decided that *Giving Instructions* was the middle course she was after. "Giving Instructions" is made up of the following steps.

1. Define what needs to be done and who should do it.
2. Tell the other person what you want him or her to do, and why.
3. Tell the other person exactly how to do what you want him or her to do, and why.
4. Ask for his or her reactions.
5. Consider his or her reactions and change your directions if appropriate.

Helen memorized these behavioral steps, and started to think about where and when she'd use them with Jim. As she rode to work on the bus that day, she "tried on" the steps, one at a time, trying hard to really imagine what she would actually say, and how Jim might react. She wanted to be sure that when she actually tried to instruct Jim on what she wanted him to do, she'd say it just right—tone of voice, not too soft and not yelling.

On Saturday, when Jim and the kids were out, she got out the little cassette recorder and recorded exactly what she thought she'd say, and then listened as openly as she could to her own words and voice. When her good friend, Lenore, came over for coffee, Helen asked her if she'd mind being a sounding board. She described what she was trying to straighten out with Jim, and how she was going to do it. Lenore listened as carefully and objectively as she could to Helen's live rehearsal, and then told her straight out what she thought Jim's reaction might be. Overall, Lenore's feedback was very positive, and Helen felt ready for the real thing. She decided to instruct Jim about some shopping that had to be done, instructions she would give him that same evening (behavioral step 1). Right after dinner that night, in a moderate tone of voice, Helen looked straight at Jim and said, "Jim, there's just too much around here for me to do all by myself, and keep my job, and shop, and whatever. We've got to share chores more. I'd really like you to stop at the supermarket on the way home from work tomorrow and get the stuff on this list, and also pick up the dry cleaning (behavioral step 2). You'd probably be best off going to the cleaner's first, and then on over to the Archway Supermarket. And see that last item on the list? Be sure to get skim, not regular (behavioral step 3). Do you see any problems in handling this (behavioral step 4)?"

Jim's first reaction was a sort of shocked surprise. But she could see he was thinking on it. The surprise faded and he said he'd do it. But he'd rather do it right then, and avoid the evening rush hour traffic tomorrow. Helen said that that would be fine (behavioral step 5). She turned away to do the dishes, with a small smile on her face from the satisfaction of a new skill, well used. She went into the kitchen, dirty dishes in hand, and started to rehearse to herself how she'd instruct Jim about sharing this chore next.

chapter ten

Assertiveness

You may look at the title of this chapter and wonder to yourself, "What do I need assertion for ... that's my problem, I'm too assertive." Before you decide to skip this chapter, read on. Many people make the mistake of confusing assertion with aggression. Nothing could be further from the truth. In fact, assertion and aggression are probably opposites. People who are properly assertive rarely resort to aggression. They don't have the need to. If you can learn to assert yourself properly, you'll feel less anger and you'll become less aggressive. How can you tell the difference between assertion and aggression? We will show you how, but first we will help you to measure your own A.Q. (Assertiveness Quotient). The A.Q. Test is very simple. Read each of the following situations and write in the letter of the response that you would actually be most likely to make if you were in that situation. We realize that you don't respond the same way all the time, even to the same situation, so pick the response that describes your most typical behavior.

THE A.Q. TEST

1. You and a friend are seated in a restaurant waiting to be served. People who came in after you are already being waited on, but you have not. The waiters keep bypassing your table without paying attention to you. What would you do?

_____

    a. Remain seated and say nothing figuring that they will get to you eventually.

    b. Angrily call out to a waiter that you were there first and if you didn't get waited on immediately you were going to leave.

    c. Get the attention of one of the waiters and calmly explain to him that you had been waiting a long time and would appreciate it if someone could take your order.

2. You are about to go shopping when one of your neighbors comes over and asks you to do her a favor and drop her off at a store that is in the opposite direction you were intending to go in. You are in a hurry and have to get home by a certain time. If you take her, it will mean that you probably will not get your own shopping done. What would you do?

_____

    a. Explain to her that you would like to help her, but that you just don't have the time right now, but you would be glad to take her some other time.

    b. Tell her you would be glad to take her, go out of your way to do it, and silently get angry at her for making you ruin your own plans.

    c. Point out to her such things as she's always bothering you to do something for her, that she never does anything for you, and that she should get her own car. Besides gas costs a lot, why should you always get stuck paying for it.

110

3. You are planning to have some friends over for dinner and would like the house to be nice and orderly. Your child tells you that he asked a friend to sleep over. You would rather he didn't do it that night because of your plans. What would you do? _____

a. Yell at your child for being so inconsiderate, tell him to send his friend home right away.

b. Explain to your child and his friend that this is not a good night to do it, that perhaps they could do it some other night soon, and maybe your child could stay at his friend's house tonight if his parents don't mind.

c. Let them stay over, because he had already asked the other child, and say nothing, while you feel taken advantage of and angry at your child for doing this to you.

4. Your spouse has made plans for the weekend without consulting you. You were hoping to spend time relaxing at home, but instead you are going to be going out with another couple that you really don't like very much. What do you do? _____

a. Go along with the plans, but sulk all night, making it quite clear to all that you are not happy. Afterwards you don't talk to your spouse for a few days, to punish him or her for ruining your weekend.

b. Refuse to go, telling your spouse that he or she has made a mess of things, so he or she will have to bear the consequences and cancel the plans.

c. Explain to your spouse that you are angry that he or she didn't consult you before making the plans, and ask him or her to please do so in the future. You go along with the plans and try to have a good time anyway, confident that you have been understood and will be treated more considerately in the future.

5. You are waiting in line to buy gasoline. You woke up early so as not to be late for work, and have been waiting a long time. Suddenly a car that has not been in

line pulls into the line in front of you. What would you do?

    a. Start honking your horn until you get his attention, then put your head out the window and threaten to kill him if he doesn't get to the end of the line. As he pulls out you yell a few choice words at him and perhaps make a gesture or two with your hands.

    b. Walk up to his car and inform him calmly that you have been waiting in line and you would appreciate it if he would go to the end of the line. If he refuses, you inform the gas station attendant of his behavior.

    c. You sit in your car and say nothing, although you are getting quite angry. You curse him out under your breath and feel helpless to do anything about the situation.

6. Your car has broken down and you take it to the dealer to have it repaired. He tells you what it will cost, but when you go to pick it up, you notice he has charged you $5.00 more than he said he would. What do you do?

    a. Call him a cheat and refuse to pay him a cent more than the quoted price. Offer to take him to court if he wants to make trouble.

    b. Call his attention to the fact that he has overcharged you and ask him why the additional charge was made. If his reason is good you pay him, otherwise you tell him why you don't feel you should have to pay.

    c. You figure it's only five dollars and you don't want to look cheap, so you pay him and say nothing. You feel cheated and tell yourself that from now on you'll just go to someone else.

7. You would like your spouse to help you with a household chore that is usually your responsibility. You don't usually ask, but you're very tired because you don't feel well and you've worked hard all day. What do you do?

a. Complain to your spouse that she or he never helps you with anything and that your marriage stinks compared to some others you know of.

b. Do it yourself, because you don't want to owe your spouse a return favor, and besides it's easier to do it yourself than to ask for help.

c. Explain the situation to your spouse and ask if she or he would help out.

8. Your boss has asked you to stay late for the third straight night. Although there are other people to ask, he always seems to ask you. This night you are supposed to go out with your mate. What would you do? _____

a. Say nothing and do as the boss asks, even though your evening will be ruined and you'll feel used and angry.

b. Explain to the boss that you've stayed late several times this week, but that you have previous plans for this evening. Ask if he could possibly ask someone else to stay this time.

c. Stay, but intentionally do a poor job to get even.

9. Your in-laws are coming over for a visit, and as usual, your kids' rooms are a mess. You always have trouble getting them to clean up. What would you do? _____

a. Yell and scream at them until they do as you ask, probably end up spanking them or threatening some dire punishment.

b. Figure it will only cause aggravation to try and get them to do it, so, as usual, you clean them yourself, letting them get away without helping.

c. Explain the situation to your children, telling them it is unfair for you to have to clean up after them, that it is one of their chores, and that if they don't do it they simply will not get any new things until they start to care properly for the things they already have.

10. Your partner would like to have sex, but you don't feel well and would rather not. In the past when you

have refused, she or he has felt rejected and it has led to arguments and bad feelings. What do you do? _____

   a. Give in and have sex, even though you will feel used and will probably not enjoy it very much.

   b. In your most affectionate way, explain that you would love to but that you really don't feel well and you hope she or he understands. Would she or he mind very much if you waited until tomorrow, you ask?

   c. Angrily explain that she or he is only interested in his or her own needs and doesn't give a damn about your feelings. Point out that this happens all the time and back it up with a few other examples of his or her inconsiderate behavior in other areas as well.

Since all the situations may not apply to you (for example, you may not have children) only score the ones that do apply to you or did in the past. The properly assertive response to each situation is listed below. Each properly assertive response is worth 5 points, the other two responses to each question are worth 0 points. Add up your total and divide by the number of questions you have answered (those that apply to you).

Properly Assertive Choices	Your Choices	Scores (5 pts each)
1. (c)	_____	_____
2. (a)	_____	_____
3. (b)	_____	_____
4. (c)	_____	_____
5. (b)	_____	_____
6. (b)	_____	_____
7. (c)	_____	_____
8. (b)	_____	_____

9. (c)   _____   _____
10. (b)   _____   _____

Total   _____

Divided by the number of items answered will give
you your Assertiveness Quotient score   _____

Let's say you have answered eight questions and have gotten the properly assertive response on five of them (remember you were not supposed to find the correct response, but rather to respond the way you would actually behave). Your total in this example would be 25 and your A.Q. would be 25 divided by 8 or 3.1 out of a possible 5.0. What does this mean? It means that you are able to assert yourself in some situations, but in a number of other situations you probably come away feeling angry, cheated, or used. If you got anything less than five, it means that there are some situations in which it would be appropriate for you to be assertive, but you are not. Take a close look at those situations where you got zeros. Is there a pattern? Do you have trouble asserting with family but not with friends? Can you assert properly with your spouse? With your children? Do you have trouble with salespeople, waiters, mechanics? Try and find the problem areas. On the other hand, if your score is less than two, you may have a general assertiveness problem. You may feel that you hardly ever do what you want or say what you want to say, and often are taken advantage of by others.

Notice that we did not distinguish between the two nonassertive responses, although you may have noticed that usually one was an aggressive response and the other a passive response. We did not distinguish between these for purposes of calculating your A.Q. because we believe that any nonassertive response can, and often does, eventually lead to aggression, although it may not be immediate and may not even involve the same situation. For example, let's look at Jim and Helen Burns again. Jim feels that Helen sides with her parents against him. The way he sees it, she often asks her parents what to do and constantly throws their opinions up to him. Last year Jim wanted to buy a small car, but her folks thought a mid-size would be safer. He wanted to send their son to camp for the summer, but her parents thought he was too young. Whenever Jim tries to argue with them, he

115

feels Helen brings up the fact that her parents are getting older and that therefore she and Jim should do as the parents say to avoid aggravating them. Jim can't think of a way of asserting himself without upsetting Helen, so he keeps it all inside and says nothing.

Sometimes, he feels that Helen must love her parents more than she loves him, but he can't tell her that because he's afraid it will make him look weak in her eyes. These feelings build up inside him like a pressure cooker, and like a pressure cooker, eventually he explodes. They end up having a fight over some minor disagreement having nothing to do with the real issues. Matters get blown out of proportion because Jim is actually angry about the in-law issues he was unable to express. If Jim had been able to assert himself to Helen and her parents, he would have defused the anger and would have felt better. Further, asserting his true feelings to Helen ("I feel that you don't love me.") would have given her a chance both to reassure him that she really does love him and to see the effect that her siding with her parents was having on him.

People sometimes think that keeping feelings inside is a good way to avoid trouble. This example shows that this just isn't true. Feelings don't simply disappear. They will build up and eventually get expressed in one way or another. Expressing them in a properly assertive way can keep them from turning into aggression.

Read each of the situations in the A.Q. Test again. Can you identify the aggressive responses? The aggressive response to each situation is listed below.

1. (b)
2. (c)
3. (a)
4. (b)
5. (a)
6. (a)
7. (a)
8. (c)
9. (a)
10. (c)

Notice the differences between the properly assertive responses and the aggressive responses. In the properly assertive response your rights are respected, but so are those of the other person. Assertion involves standing up for your own rights, without stepping on the rights of others. The basis of assertion is that everyone is entitled to be treated with consideration and respect, including yourself. The passive individual hurts him or herself, the aggressive individual hurts others. The assertive individual tries to avoid hurting anyone.

The ten situations making up the A.Q. Test should give you a good idea of what kinds of behavior are involved in assertiveness. A properly assertive person should be able to:

1. Express him or herself firmly and clearly without having to scream, raise his or her voice, resort to foul language or threats.
2. Ask friends, relatives, and others for help or favors.
3. Refuse to do something that is unreasonable when asked by others. (This doesn't mean that one should never go out of his or her way to do a favor. Only that one should be able to refuse if there is a good reason for such a refusal.)
4. Stand up for his or her rights.
5. Give and receive compliments without embarrassment.
6. Admit that he or she is wrong.

In order to help you to become a properly assertive individual, we must first look at what stops people from asserting themselves. Why do we allow ourselves to be overcharged without complaining about it? Why can't we tell the neighbor that it is impossible to drive her across town today? There are several reasons for nonassertive behavior.

1. Many people feel they are worthless and undeserving. They don't like or respect themselves very much and don't expect others to either. In short, they don't feel they are worth standing up for.
2. Some people simply don't know what to say. They don't know what the assertive response is.
3. Others get very nervous when it comes to speaking up. Anxiety stops them from asserting themselves.
4. There are also those who feel that trouble will be avoided if they keep everything inside and don't make waves.

We have already discussed the fourth point and seen that it simply isn't true. You are not doing anyone, including yourself, a favor if you hold your feelings in. If you don't tell your neighbor that you simply can't do that favor today, you will probably end up resenting her later and hurting your friendship even more than refusing to do the favor would have. People are usually more understanding than we think, especially if we present our reasons in an honest, friendly, and direct way. Similarly, if you agree to have sex when you really don't feel like it in order to avoid a fight with your spouse, your feelings of resentment over having been used will probably cause you to express your anger in some other hurtful way, which will probably hurt your relationship more than an honest and considerate refusal to have sex would have. Assertiveness is also inhibited when people don't respect themselves enough.

FEELINGS OF WORTHLESSNESS

A surprisingly large number of people don't really like themselves very much. They feel insecure and inadequate. Since they often feel worthless, they can't see much reason why other people would want them for friends, or even for relatives. Why can't people refuse unreasonable requests made by others? One reason might be that they are afraid that the other person only likes them for selfish reasons. My neighbor won't like me unless I always do things for her. My child will only love me if I give in to everything he or she wants. My boss only keeps me on the job because I do everything he asks without question. These are common feelings that people have, feelings which seem to say: "People only like, need, or want me for what I can do for them." Why do we have these insecurities or feelings of worthlessness? In most cases, such feelings have developed over a long period of time. Perhaps your parents criticized you too much or failed to praise you enough when you did something good. Maybe you didn't do as well in school or in sports as your siblings and friends. You might have had some faults (perhaps you were considerably overweight) which people focused on instead of your good qualities. It is possible that your spouse continues to devalue your good qualities (you don't make as much money as Bill; you don't cook as well as his mother). It's hard to say where these feelings came from, but the more important question is how to get rid of them? How can you feel good about yourself?

People often have *internal rules* (beliefs), which they use to judge themselves and others. Doctors are better than plumbers, adults are better than children, teachers are better than students, rich people are better than poor people, employed people are better than unemployed people, men are better than women, are but a few examples of this arbitrary way of thinking. Where do we get such ideas? Where is this master list kept? Who made it up? People are only people, regardless of what they do and what they have, and as people, we are all equally worthwhile and valuable. A short example may make this a little clearer. While doing therapy, one of the authors was working with a client who felt especially worthless. The following discussion helped to point out how unnecessary such self-devaluation is.

Therapist: So you would say that I am worth more as a person than you are.
    Client: Absolutely.
Therapist: Tell me why I am worth more.
    Client: You have an important job, you help others, you have more money. I don't even have a job.
Therapist: And what if there was a financial crisis and this clinic had to fire me in order to save money . . . would I still be more valuable than you?
    Client: Certainly.
Therapist: But I wouldn't have my important job, I wouldn't be helping people, and I would soon run out of money.
    Client: But you would still be you. You wouldn't change just because you lost your job.
Therapist: So these other things, a job and money, don't really matter. As a person I would be just as worthwhile as anyone else, just as you are.
    Client: I'm beginning to see your point.

The idea that some people are better than others is really an irrational one and makes little logical sense, yet a great many people often behave as if they believed it were unquestionably true. Just as we suggested in discussing the effects of positive self-statements on self-control (Chapter 3), whenever you begin to feel badly about yourself, it may help to have a little logical conversation with yourself in which you express such positive sentiments as "I'm as good as anyone else" or "nobody is better (or for that matter worse) than I am" or "I deserve to be treated with as much respect as anyone else" or "my rights are as important as others' are."

    People who have poor self-images often fall into a pattern of emphasizing the negative about themselves. All people have good features as well as bad ones. Nobody is perfect, and although we should always try to be the best we can, we shouldn't set perfection as our goal. (There's a difference between striving to be good and demanding to be perfect.) Since we all have both good or bad features, it is largely our choice whether we emphasize the good or the bad. We all know people who think they are wonderful. We see their faults, but they never seem to, and as a result, they usually feel pretty good about themselves. While this is as incorrect as seeing only the negative, it is not destructive, but rather has a positive effect. While most of us have been taught that bragging and vanity are undesirable qualities, critical, self-deprecating behavior is equally undesirable, and much more harmful. The ideal is a balance: recognition of both one's good qualities and one's faults. In the past the faults were given the emphasis, now it is necessary to give the positive equal time.

The following exercise is a simple way to begin working on your feelings of self-worth. Try to think of some positive things to say about yourself. They don't have to be earthshaking. You might say, for example, that you're a good bowler, that you like children, that you have a good sense of humor, or that you keep the house clean. It may not come easy at first but keep trying. Take an index card and write down five or six positive things about yourself, then put it in a convenient and visible place (your wallet, near the phone, on your desk) and make a point of looking at it several times a day. What about those negative qualities that you probably still feel are more important? Take another card and write down the two or three things you feel are your worst qualities. If you examine them, you might find that they are not permanent, unchangeable characteristics, but rather are probably things that you have been doing. This is an important difference, as they are things you have been doing, *not* things that you are. If they are things that you have been doing, they are probably things that you can stop doing if you want to badly enough.

Let's take Barbara Parks and her son as an example. As a result of the problems she has had with Tom, Barbara thinks she is a lousy mother, and this makes her feel very negatively about herself (she's no good as a person, because she's such a lousy mother). If we ask Barbara to list her most negative feature, she would no doubt tell us that she is a lousy mother. Let's pick up the conversation between us and Barbara at this point:

   Us: What makes you a lousy mother?
Barbara: Everything.
   Us: Don't you love your son?
Barbara: Of course!
   Us: And haven't you always tried to care for him as best you could?
Barbara: Certainly. I'd do anything to help him.
   Us: That doesn't sound very much like a terrible mother.
Barbara: But I yell at him all the time.
   Us: So it's not that you're a lousy mother, it's that you yell at him too much.
Barbara: I guess so.
   Us: Well that sounds like something you might be able to change.

This example is meant to make two points. First, that I am a lousy this or a terrible that are "global put downs," conclusions that we draw based on something we are doing. It is necessary to get behind such statements and sort out the behavior we are really concerned about. "I am a lousy mother" sounds like a permanent condition. It really stands for "I yell at my son too much," which can more easily be worked on. That is the second point, that we can work to change those things about ourselves that we don't like.

  Take the card with the negative items and try to sort out what you really don't like. Take the global statements (the "I am's") and try to convert them to specific behaviors (the "I do's"). Then make a list of the possible ways that you can start to change some of those unwanted behaviors. The chapters of this book provide methods for changing many of the behaviors you may not like. Whenever you find yourself thinking negatively about yourself, sort out what you don't like and add the statement "but I can (and will) change that." Remember the list of positive qualities and try to give them equal time. Emphasize the positive; work to change the negative. Doing these things will have a positive effect on your self-respect and your sense of being a worthwhile person. As you come to feel better about yourself, you will be more able to be assertive wherever and whenever it is appropriate.

KNOWING WHAT TO SAY

We often hear people complain that they don't know what the properly assertive response is. There are at least two parts to the assertive response: what to say, and how to say it. (*What to say* refers to the actual content of what you say [the words].) Take another look at the A.Q. Test. The assertive responses are examples of the type of response that is appropriate. In each case the response is a fair (to you and the other person), firm and direct explanation or a statement of feelings.

Study the A.Q. Test until you get the idea of the types of responses that are considered properly assertive. It is, of course, impossible to give examples of every situation you will ever confront, so we have provided only a general sampling. Likewise, it is impossible for us to give you the exact words you will need to assert yourself in the wide variety of situations that will require assertion. We suggest that you begin to take notice of the kinds of assertive statements you hear other people make. Being a careful observer of assertive models is a good way to build your own assertiveness responses. When you hear a good assertive statement, practice saying it to yourself first, say it out loud a few times, and then try it with others in situations that are appropriate. It may also help to ask other people, like your friend or spouse, what they would say in this situation.

What you say is important, but so is *how* you say it. People who are properly assertive, look and act assertively as well. Here are a few rules that may help you.

1. Look other people in the eye. It tells them you feel good about yourself, you feel you are as good as they are, and have nothing to feel ashamed of or apologize for. People like it when you make eye contact.
2. Stand up straight. Your posture says something about your feelings about yourself.
3. Speak in a firm, strong voice, loudly enough to be easily heard, but don't yell or overpower the other person.

DEALING WITH ANXIETY

Assertiveness also often fails to occur when it should because the idea of actually standing up for oneself causes the person to become tense and anxious. They would rather lose five dollars than tell the mechanic he is overcharging them. They would rather fail a course than question the teacher's grading of their exam. Anxiety can be dealt with in several ways. You can use relaxation, which is described in Chapter 2. This is a most effective way of reducing anxiety and it can be used to facilitate assertive behavior. We strongly recommend that you learn the relaxation techniques well and begin to use them in assertive situations.

It may also help to examine what it is you are afraid of. What do you think will happen if you question the mechanic's bill? Again, let's tune in on a typical conversation with a client who has this particular assertion problem.

Therapist: What do you think will happen if you ask him what the overcharge is for?

Client: I don't know. I never thought about it.

Therapist: Do you think he'd hit you?

Client: Of course not. He'd risk getting arrested.

Therapist: Well. What then?

Client: I guess I'd feel cheap.

Therapist: But it was he that was cheating you. He should feel cheap.

Client: True. But I'm sure he wouldn't.

Therapist: So what if he thought you were cheap. Is that terrible?

Client: I guess not. It wouldn't mean I was cheap.

Therapist: Exactly. Besides, should you let what someone else thinks keep you from standing up for your rights?

Client: Certainly not.

In this, as in most cases, the actual consequences are not nearly as ominous as the feared consequences. Simply thinking about what will realistically happen may serve to reduce some of the anxiety. Our fears often center on what we expect others might think about us. These others are usually strangers who we will never see again anyway, yet we act as though they will have nothing better to do than go around telling everyone about us. In reality, people usually have more respect for the person who asserts him or herself than for the nonassertive person. As you begin to show respect for yourself, you will begin to notice others respecting you more also.

Following are the key questions to ask yourself in each situation.

1. What am I really afraid of?
2. How likely is that to happen, realistically?
3. Why would that be so terrible?

Thinking about things in this way make them less anxiety provoking and, combined with relaxation, may increase your ability to assert yourself properly.

TO ASSERT OR NOT ASSERT?

That is the question, which may be a surprising question, especially at the end of a chapter devoted to encouraging you to become properly assertive. Our goals in this chapter have been to enable you to assert yourself when you want to and to help you to distinguish between assertion and aggression. In most situations, a properly assertive response will be the most beneficial for all concerned, but a realistic evaluation of each situation must be made as well. Take the example involving the boss and working late (A.Q. Test, situation 8). You might have said to yourself that the assertive response might be a good way to lose your job. We suggested that you calmly explain the situation to your boss and *ask* if other arrangements might be made. This should work well with any reasonable person, but your boss might not be all that reasonable. We might still suggest asserting your position to him, but with the qualifier that if he did not see your point, it might be to your advantage to re-evaluate your position. We would not recommend that you continue to assert yourself by refusing to work if it means losing your job. It is important to be able to assert yourself when you want to, but it is not a catastrophe to decide that it would be better for you not to assert yourself in certain situations. In most situations, however, a properly assertive response will be more likely to avoid future trouble, especially of an aggressive nature, than to cause it.

Suggested Readings

We expect there will be readers of this book who will wish to learn more about the methods we have discussed, and their roots in psychology. The books listed below are, we feel, an excellent collection for this purpose. They are informative, clearly written source materials to which we are pleased to refer you.

Chapter 1: Introduction

Goldstein, A.P., Carr, E., Davidson, W., and Wehr, P., *In Response to Aggression: Methods of Control and Constructive Alternatives.* New York: Pergamon, Press, 1981.

Johnson, R.N., *Aggression in Man and Animals.* Philadelphia: W.B. Saunders, 1972.

Chapter 2: Relaxation

Benson, H., *The Relaxation Response.* New York: Avon, 1975.

Walker, C.E., *Learn to Relax.* Englewood Cliffs, N.J.: Prentice-Hall, 1975.

Chapter 3: Self-Control

Ellis, A., and Harper, R.A., *A New Guide to Rational Living.* No. Hollywood, Calif.: Wilshire Book Co., 1976.

Novaco, N.W., *Anger Control.* Lexington, Mass.: Lexington Books, 1975.

Chapter 4: Calming Others

Filley, A.C., *Interpersonal Conflict Resolution.* Glenview, Ill.: Scott, Foresman & Co., 1974.

Goldstein, A.P., Monti, P.J., Sardino, T.J., and Green, D.J., *Police Crisis Intervention.* New York: Pergamon Press, 1979.

Chapter 5: Constructive Communication

Wahlroos, S., *Family Communication.* New York: Macmillan, 1974.

Egan, G., *Interpersonal Living.* Monterey, Calif.: Brooks/Cole, 1976.

Chapter 6: Negotiation

Ilich, J., *The Art and Skill of Successful Negotiation.* Englewood Cliffs, N.J.: Prentice-Hall, 1973.

Karlins, M., and Abelson, H.I., *Persuasion.* New York: Springer, 1970.

Chapter 7: Contracting

DeRisi, W.J., and Butz, G., *Writing Behavioral Contracts.* Champaign, Ill.: Research Press, 1975.

Dardig, J.C., and Heward, W.L., *Sign Here: A Contracting Book for Children and Their Parents.* Kalamazoo, Mich.: Behaviordelia, 1976.

Chapter 8: Rewards and Nonaggressive Punishment

Watson, D.L., and Tharp, R.G., *Self-Directed Behavior: Self-Modification for Personal Adjustment.* (3rd ed.) Monterey, Calif.: Brooks Cole, 1980.

Watson, L.S. *Child Behavior Modification.* New York: Pergamon Press, 1973.

Chapter 9: Positive Skill Bulding

Goldstein, A.P., Sprafkin, R.P., and Gershaw, N.J., *I Know What's*

Wrong, But I Don't Know What to Do About It. Englewood Cliffs, N.J.: Prentice-Hall, 1979.

Liberman, R.P., King, L.W., DeRisi, W.J., and McCann, M., *Personal Effectiveness.* Champaign, Ill: Research Press, 1975.

Chapter 10: Assertiveness

Alberti, R.E. & Emmons, M.L., *Your Perfect Right.* San Luis Obispo, Calif.: Impact, 1974.

Bower, S.A., and Bower, G.H., *Asserting Yourself.* Reading, Mass.: Addison-Wesley, 1979.

Index

A